HOW TO KILL A NARCISSIST

DEBUNKING THE MYTH OF NARCISSISM AND RECOVERING FROM NARCISSISTIC ABUSE

JH SIMON

This book is not intended as a substitute for legal, medical or mental health advice. The intent of this book is to provide general advice on the topic matter covered. If professional advice or expert assistance is required, it should be sought out.

ISBN: 9781520117676

Contents

The penny drops

Man is free at the moment he wishes to be.

- Voltaire

The fact that you're reading this book means you're onto something. Maybe a particular event burst the bubble and a small gap opened up as a result. A gap in what, you're not sure, but you felt it. It happened when a significant person in your life went that little bit too far, and you finally said to yourself: 'This is not normal. Why am I tolerating this crap?' You didn't really know what normal was, but you knew that the union which you have with this person is definitely not it.

Through this small gap which opened up, you may have begun to realise some or all of the following about your relationship:

- **It's unbalanced:** The other person seems to have the upper hand and the final say, and you have to struggle to get an equal footing with them. Their problems get top priority. When you try to express or assert yourself, the other person finds a way to subdue you and bring the focus back onto them.

- **It's manipulative:** Like being under a spell, the other person seems to have an uncanny ability to pull your strings and get their way with you. Often you don't want them to, but it just happens. When you try to influence them in any way, you're met with so many obstacles you give up.

- **It's intrusive:** They have a permanent place in your mind. There doesn't seem to be any psychological separation between you and them, and they enter your emotional space effortlessly. You find yourself craving some separation and psychological 'air', but end up feeling enormous guilt. Being a distinct individual in control of your destiny does not feel like an option with them in your life.

- **It's rigid:** You don't experience much growth from the relationship, and it doesn't go anywhere fast. It feels ritualistic, and you wish there were more to it.

- **It's exhausting:** You walk on eggshells around that person. There's no particular reason. Simply being around them makes you anxious, like you don't quite stack up and you have to prove yourself to them.

- **It's oppressive:** It's taken for granted that the other person is superior to you. Spending time with them leaves you with a hopeless sense of inferiority.

- **It's hollow:** The relationship feels empty and sad, and you don't get much emotional nourishment from it.
- **It's perplexing:** You can never seem to find solid ground. There's always a drama which must be addressed or something which the other person is unhappy about that you feel you need to fix. You crave peace and security, but it somehow always eludes you.
- **It sucks you in:** There seems to be an invisible force which sucks you toward the other person. Even when you disconnect for a while, all it takes is a simple question to draw you back in and distract you from your task. You feel powerless to resist this emotional force, which seems to take on a life of its own.

Then one thing leads to another, and you find yourself googling 'Narcissistic Personality Disorder'. You read a few articles, and your jaw drops. After the initial shock wears off, you investigate further. You read the forums, and you realise that a countless number of people share your experience. You learn the lingo; gas-lighting, idealise, devalue, discard, triangulation, hoovering and baiting. You put the pieces together and begin to see that many of these tactics have been done to you at some stage. It's like your life story is being told to you. You begin to wonder: can this be true? Do people like this really exist? You read on. Finally, it hits you with full force. You realise that you're not crazy; what you've been experiencing all this time is definitely real. People like this do exist. Not only do they exist in the world, they exist in *your* world. You don't know whether to laugh or cry. You feel rage, sadness and despair, and a little bit of relief. You walk around with a sense of lightness, but also with a sense of having been stained somehow. Your entire reality has been turned on its head. You start questioning your core instincts. You realise that the relationship dynamics which you accepted and took as gospel are both unhealthy and grossly manipulative. You start to look at people differently. You monitor their behaviour, even that of the people you have known for years or a lifetime. The picture is not entirely clear. What *is* clear, however, is that you have a problem with *narcissists* and you're only just waking up to it.

Down the rabbit hole

What you might not have realised is that monitoring the behaviours of others, while important, is not enough. Staying on the surface will only serve to get you mixed up in drama after drama and will keep you guessing as to what's normal and what's narcissistic. The crucial thing to realise is that the tactics which you have been subjected to are just the tip of the problem; it goes much deeper. The *core* of the problem is often much harder to see.

Also, if you think it's as simple as walking away, guess again: The way out is not an actual road which leads to a new life and exciting adventures. You might have already suspected this. It was not a coincidence that you found yourself in this position to begin with. You are still carrying the same beliefs, behaviours and paradigms. You can walk away from a partner, or distance yourself from certain family members, choose a new set of friends, or quit a job, but in time you'll end up in the arms of another narcissist, or eventually back under the control of the same narcissist. To make lasting changes, you will need a strategy.

Sharpen your sword

As the title points out, this book is a 101 on how to kill a narcissist. No, we're not discussing actual murder! This is about understanding the core of the problem, not just the symptoms. It's about seeing the core of the problem in the narcissist, and the core of the problem in you. This is about becoming conscious of what makes you a target for narcissists. It's about shifting your paradigms so you can begin to separate yourself from the problem. It's also about obtaining new internal resources which narcissists don't want you to develop, mainly because these resources make you less susceptible to their control. It's about developing a new belief set. It's about educating yourself, and as a result, empowering yourself. It's about developing your own autonomous identity, free of shame and guilt; a fortress which nobody will be able to access without your explicit permission and unless they offer you the due respect. With time, your new resources and beliefs will allow you to hop over to the sunny, narcissism-free side of the street. So in a way, yes, we are going to kill some narcissists. More specifically, we're going to starve them to death by taking away their narcissistic supply. And it all starts with you.

First things first

Terms such as Narcissistic Personality Disorder (NPD), Sociopath, Psychopath and Narcopath are the labels typically associated with narcissism. With extreme levels of narcissism, it can be helpful to have such labels. Violent, destructive and acutely manipulative people should be placed in a pigeonhole to remind us that only physical distance can protect us from them. Dealing with the most violent and sadistic of narcissists is beyond the scope of this book, however. Being forced to go no contact, restraining orders and post-traumatic stress disorder are not light topics. Personality disorders and domestic abuse are also beyond the scope of this book. Professional help should be sought when dealing with such issues.

Most narcissists sit more in the middle band, and at first glance seem harmless. The damage done by your average narcissist seeps in like a slow acting poison. Being in a relationship with a narcissist causes untold damage, without them necessarily swindling you of all your money or becoming violent. A lot of narcissists subject their target to the slow, painful death by narcissism - without criminal intent. They do most of their damage through emotional abuse, by shaming and manipulating their target to enforce control.

This book focuses on the *narcissist archetype*. This archetype applies to the father or mother who fills their own needs by objectifying their children and keeping them both subjugated and trapped in a psychological cage. It applies to the friend who loves having weaker people around just so they can ridicule them and feel powerful around them, as well as feed off them for narcissistic supply. It relates to the lover who objectifies and keeps their partner trapped in an agonising emotional storm. It applies to the boss who charms, controls, frightens and objectifies his employees with the intention of reinforcing their power in the workplace. This book focuses on narcissism as not only an archetype but also as a *regime;* a structure with strict rules aimed at objectifying and subjugating others for narcissistic supply. This book tries to leave the popular labels and theory behind so that the heart and soul of narcissism can be clearly seen without the external layers to muddy the view.

For the sake of simplicity, the term narcissist will be employed in this book. Narcissist regime will refer to the structure between two or more people where a person controls others and extracts narcissistic supply, either through a position of power such as parenthood or a management position or through emotional manipulation in a relationship. Often it is a combination of both, where a position of power gives a narcissist the licence to control their target and emotional manipulation enforces the control on a more personal level.

On the other hand, the target of the narcissist will not be given a special label, since that would pigeonhole them and define them in comparison to the narcissist, hence keeping them trapped in the game. The entire purpose of this book is to assist the targets of narcissism in breaking free, reminding them that their identity does indeed exist outside of a narcissist regime and encourages them to define their identity and self-worth according to their own choosing. Again, for the sake of simplicity, the term target will be used in combination with you, which addresses the reader as a person who can relate to the content. This provides us with a useful label that is not based on subjugation or a role. Anybody can be a target of something. Being so does not influence one's identity.

Lastly, it is crucial that we view narcissism itself as the enemy, and not designate specific people as evil. Although extremely difficult in some cases, hatred for the narcissist keeps us stuck and leads to us surrendering our personal power. We must remember that beneath the behaviours and beliefs we are all human beings. It is specifically this humanity in us which is the gateway to a life of strength and peace and which separates us from the perils of narcissism. Furthermore, narcissism can be handed down for generations and be so ingrained in the family dynamic that there is no awareness by anybody that it is going on, including the narcissist. Many people learnt narcissism through abuse from a parent or loved one. It is also argued that some people are simply born with a reduced capacity for shame, and narcissism as well as manipulation are a natural outcome of this. To top it all off, we need to remember that we are all capable of narcissism if we stray too far from our inherent humanity.

Make no mistake, narcissism is a horrible thing. But the finger should be kept pointed solely at the disease, and never the person. Yes, how you treat a person will change when they exhibit narcissistic behaviours, but as this book will explain, once we have identified narcissistic tendencies in a person, the next step will be to bring the focus away from that person and then inward into ourselves, where change can happen.

The enduring effects of life under a narcissist regime

Paul has a recurring nightmare where he is trapped in an underground cave with hot flames all around him. An intense feeling of claustrophobia shakes his core, and he wakes up in terror, gasping for air. He realises he is having a panic attack. It feels like being in purgatory; an unbearable, infinite fear which he tries desperately to escape but cannot find a way out. He scrambles to switch the light on and then starts pacing up and down his apartment trying to shake it off. He rushes down the stairs and out into the chilly morning air. It helps a bit. It takes over an hour for the feeling of panic to dissipate. He has no idea why he keeps having dreams like this.

Cindy is an intelligent, pleasant girl. Her broken smile hints at the sadness inside, but she is polite and acts happy enough, so people don't stick their noses into her business. She obediently obliges most requests, tends to agree with most opinions and goes along with most of the plans of others. She's simply there, and people can trust her not to rock the boat.

Igor is 34 years old, but people think he's 25. He's a dreamer. He'd like to be in a band, or maybe write the next great novel. He's not sure which. He never felt capable enough or smart enough to act on his dreams. To make matters worse, he feels trapped working in a call centre. Also, he's been with his girlfriend Anna on and off for 4 years now. Every time they fight, Igor threatens to leave but is met with tears and threats of suicide. The guilt is overwhelming, and he stays. He wants desperately to leave the relationship but can't see a way out.

After an intense summer romance, Noah asked Ariana to marry him. She said yes. Noah was a dream come true. He was attentive, he focused all of his energy on Ariana, shared in her dreams and was ready to commit. They got married in a simple ceremony. Soon after the wedding, things started to change. Noah became critical of Ariana, and flew into a rage if she came home any later than the expected time. Ariana had seen that rage in small doses before the wedding but had disregarded it, especially when Noah apologised swiftly with his boyish desperation. Noah was grandiose and insisted that everything he did was far superior to anyone else. He loved having the attention on himself and would tell endless stories to any willing audience without ever showing interest in the listener. He had a certain charm about him, so most people tolerated him. Ariana was deeply dissatisfied with the relationship and tired of Noah's rage, which came out randomly and without any real reason. After fourteen years, three children and having left most of her friends behind, she was far too daunted by the idea of leaving and starting again.

Why me? Qualifying as a target

Get em' while they're young

As children, we are curious, sensitive, vulnerable, and of course, impressionable, absorbing everything around us like sponges as the core of how we relate to others is formed. We worship the people who are responsible for us. Our helplessness means we have no choice but to give them absolute power. With that power, they have the potential to either lead us toward a life of independence or to use us for their own ego supply. Narcissists choose the latter.

This position of power obviously begins with parents but can also apply to uncles and aunties, family friends, teachers or sports coaches. For the narcissist, having impressionable young people looking up to them heightens their sense of power. They get to play out their shameless 'wise leader' role at the expense of the child. They feel that their position of power gives them a license to judge, control and belittle the child if the child does not meet their expectations. In their grandiose mind, they can take advantage of the responsibility bestowed upon them by using it as a way to feed their ego.

The dangerous (and sad) thing is that it lies outside of the child's conscious awareness. It happened at a time when they had little of it. True awareness begins in adulthood. When vulnerable and dependent, the child can unwittingly become an object of narcissistic supply, and not really be aware of what is happening. When it's done long enough, it can become as normal as the air they breathe. The child is manipulated and groomed into a role of perpetual worship and dependence.

Leadership is about showing others the path so they can walk it, outgrow it and then eventually forge their own path. Narcissists in leadership hold back the target from differentiating by supporting the child only within the constraints of the relationship, and only as long as the child is fulfilling their role by providing narcissistic supply. The narcissist projects their ego needs onto the child, and rather than put their needs aside to help the child grow, expects the child to adapt to *them* instead. This role reversal is the core of a narcissist-child relationship, which leads to arrested development in the child and grooms them to be more susceptible to narcissism. The child grows up believing that relationships are about playing their role and adapting to the needs of others. It's one of the greatest lies told to some children; that dependence is a fact of life and that it never ends. This lie can continue throughout adulthood.

The ideal target

Some people could have unwittingly fallen into a narcissist regime from a young age, and/or they could be an emotionally sensitive person. *Empaths*, as they are referred to:

- are intuitive and possess high emotional intelligence
- experience their emotions with a very high intensity, which often debilitates and severely stunts the ability for rational thought
- can sense and are very attuned to the emotions of others, even going as far as to take on these emotions, which can quickly drain the Empath's energy if they are not careful
- are good listeners and can sacrifice their attention for long periods of time
- have a very strong craving to connect with others emotionally, which is often stronger than reason and common sense
- have more difficulty than others in keeping up with daily life, and so are more prone to seeking out a higher power for guidance and support

- can more easily be influenced than others

The emotional world of an Empath is very rich. They are artists and dreamers. They inspire others with their energy and zest for life. They are healers, and usually very creative and spiritual. They can brighten up a person's day just by being themselves. Yet this richness comes with a cost:

- Empaths crave love and connection more than most people, and they suffer when isolated. As a result of this deep need for emotional connection, their boundaries are usually weak.
- The emotional buttons of an Empath are easier to push than those of Non-Empaths. Because they have a super sensitive emotional antenna, even the smallest attack can shake them up. When somebody else shows intense emotion, whether it be anger, sadness or outrage, the Empath feels like they are being engulfed and bombarded. With that, their immune system drops and their anxiety increases.
- They often feel fatigued, just by being around people. They get sick more easily. They are often nervous and afraid. It has nothing to do with strength; inside their body and mind, they are simply overwhelmed with fear, shame and anxiety. This deafening, blinding emotional system makes it hard to see out into the world.

- Empaths must have structure at all times. They need an environment which insulates them so that emotions don't get out of hand.

For all of the above reasons, Empaths are perfect targets for narcissists. Their inner beauty, weak boundaries, compromised internal strength and strong need for connection make them a gold mine of narcissistic supply. To get the upper hand, the narcissist only has to bombard the emotional system of the Empath and then coerce the Empath into cooperating with their demands.

A high degree of skill and support is required to manage the often tumultuous inner world of the Empath properly. In many families, especially conservative, traditional or abusive ones, the need of the Empath to be deeply understood and supported can be neglected. Even worse, especially for men, they can be shamed for their 'softness'. These unmet needs and an inability to weather their emotional storm can leave the Empath with low self-esteem and an overwhelming craving for love, and not really be aware why. The narcissist will smell this like a shark smells blood and swoop in. The charm of the narcissist can be intoxicating and irresistible to the Empath. The narcissist can offer the Empath structure, even though that structure is oppressive and mostly benefits the narcissist.

Identifying with being an Empath and/or with being born into a narcissist regime can help you understand how your origins have impacted your life so far, and can also remind you that it's not your fault. Most importantly, it can help you draw a line and make the decision to take your future into your own hands. Where you go from here is entirely within your power.

Mortal Gods

Glory, built on selfish principles, is shame and guilt.

- William Cowper

The parental emotion

Humanity is eternally growing and improving. We are becoming exponentially more innovative and self-aware. Olympic world records are broken and re-broken over and over again. Technology and healthcare have improved our quality of life immeasurably. Music and art are evolving in exciting and beautiful ways. We are constantly discovering more about the mind and about our universe. Therapeutic methods keep coming and improving.

Inside all of us is a power which wants to expand and improve. This force gives us grand images of being bigger and better than we currently are. It's not there by accident; life has an agenda. It wants to evolve. For this reason, we are born with an inherent *grandeur*. This is an inner sense of specialness which we can tap into and which can spur us to both create and to become more than we are. Grandeur is deeply personal and spiritual. It tells us we are capable of *anything*. It is an upward, outward and infinite force. It is our innate creativity and connection to the god realm.

Related to this is *grandiosity*. Grandiosity is one person's grandeur in comparison to another's. It is ego based. It makes us want to be bigger and better than other people. It pits us against one another. Anybody who has ever received a first place prize or has been given something for free while everyone else paid knows how satisfying grandiosity feels. It is rising above the crowd and beyond the usual standard. It's about *achieving more* and *being more* than others.

Life also wants us to coexist. Unchecked, grandiosity can be an ugly thing. If we are all blindly following our grandiose instincts, we could destroy ourselves and each other in an attempt to rise to the top. Men such as Adolf Hitler and Pablo Escobar had uncontrollable grandiosity. One desired world domination and the other sought nothing less than unlimited power and money. As a result, mass murder for them became 'collateral damage'. Life cannot tolerate such a blatant lack of humanity; it needs balance. Luckily, for most of us, there's an opposing force which keeps our grandiosity in check: Shame.

Shame is an unpleasant emotion. At its mildest, it's a slight ache in the chest and a loss of vigour and energy. At its most potent, it physically deflates you – your head sinks into your shoulders, your shoulders slump and your body crumples. It emotionally stunts you – your brain feels foggy and sluggish, you question yourself, you lose heart, you hold back your feelings and opinions. It's an emotion which reduces your mental capacity – you draw a blank and can't think or come up with any ideas. It temporarily exiles you from the world - you feel overexposed with a desperate need to hide from others. It creates a dark, introspective, confined space in your psyche where nothing else can enter. It brings you face to face with yourself, where you can see all your flaws and spots up close. It makes you painfully aware of the fact that you are limited and not as god-like as you sometimes feel. It is the parent who tells you 'no' and 'go to your room'.

The normalising power of shame

This 'psychological timeout' exists for three main reasons:

- To remind you that although you have the capacity for grandiosity, you are a human being in a human body, living in a human world. Your influence and ability only go so far, and your environment can only accommodate you so much.

- To give you the time and space for self-reflection and to make adjustments if needed.
- To balance the social hierarchy. When one person in a group exhibits more power and grandiosity than the others, shame will cut down the grandiosity of the others to ensure balance is achieved. Alternatively, if a person demonstrates their power and grandiosity and is cut down by another member who feels threatened, shame will arise to compensate. This balancing act is designed to encourage conformity and unity and ensures that the boat is not rocked too much.

Shame effectively functions on two fronts:

- **Personal:** Personal shame arises when you envision a particular reality for yourself but come up short. For example, when you cannot afford your dream vacation or if you wish you were taller (or shorter).
- **Social:** Environmental shame is based on the people around you, such as being too loud and being given a disapproving stare by a loved one or when somebody else has more money than you.

If you aim high for yourself and fall short, shame will remind you that you are not there yet and need to improve. If your environment does not tolerate your needs, wants and expressions of self, shame will kick in to warn you that what you are doing and who you are at that moment is threatening to those who you value.

Fit in, play nice. Measure up, get it right

Clearly, shame is not just about being too big for your britches. It's about living up to the standards set by the people in your life and society as a whole. Imagine a child sitting with their family, who are all eating chocolate, but being told that they cannot have any until they are older. Everyone is enjoying their delicious chocolate, savouring each bite and sharing opinions about what they like most about it. Now imagine the child sitting there, observing this, wanting desperately to join in, but being told sternly by father or mother that it's not going to happen. The child will not only feel held back but also inferior. Shame will wash over them. The child will feel the harsh reality of wanting but instead falling short. They will feel the agony of not measuring up to the people who they value. This is a very painful experience.

Figure 1: *Shame is encountered when your limits are smaller than that of another person*

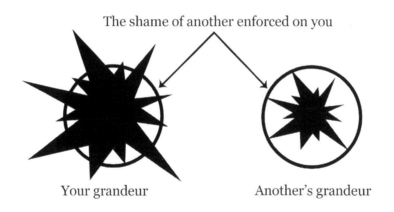

Figure 2: *You will also encounter shame when the expression of your grandeur is not accepted by another person*

Everybody can recall times when they saw others have it better, and as a result began to feel inferior. A standard was set which they valued and wanted to meet. For example, you may wish to lose weight. One day, your friend explains with great joy how they managed to shed 6 kilograms in the last month. You instantly start looking inside yourself to consider how far you are with your weight loss. Your reality narrows down, and you start to think about what you can do to achieve the same thing. You blurt out something like 'Yes, I'm signing up for the gym soon. My target is 10 kilograms by the end of the year'. Your shame has kicked in.

The more you look at it, the more you see how shame aims to bind society together. Depending on the situation, it will either cut you down or spur you to grow and improve. It doesn't want every person to walk around believing they are royalty nor does it want people to fall too far behind the pack. It wants the herd to achieve balance and harmony, to behave according to the rules and to live up to the standards set by others. It wants us to do what the majority are doing; to act, feel and behave like other human beings.

Shame activates in countless ways. For example:

Scenario	Shame reaction
Your colleagues are socialising together and you're sitting alone	"I feel like a freak sitting alone"
You're laughing uncontrollably, until your mother or father gives you a sharp stare and tells you to stop	Your excitement drops. "I should act civil and respect that others are threatened/annoyed by commotion."
A group of people are sitting together laughing, and you and your friends are sitting there quietly.	"They're having fun, why aren't we?"
You see a poster of a supermodel and start comparing yourself to her/him	"I'm just an ordinary person, look how amazing they are"
A friend tells you about their spectacular weekend socialising and drinking, then asks you what you did, which you answer "Just had lunch with the family and watched television"	You question your social life. "Look how much fun everyone else having. My life is boring"
You tell your parent with great excitement about your new job promotion, but they don't react with much enthusiasm	Your enthusiasm and excitement drops measurably and you begin to question how great your promotion really is.

Right or wrong, shame wants us to fall into line. It tells us that we don't measure up and we should improve/adapt in order to fit in. It says we've gone too far and that we need to tone things down. It tells us that there is a finite amount of power in our group, and if we push any harder we will threaten the balance. It tells us to make room for others. It teaches us that we are not gods and that we live in a society. Not only does it aim to keep our grandiosity in check, but it also aims to keep us unified. If our needs, wants and expressions threaten or separate us too much from the tribe, then it will threaten our place in the group. We are programmed to believe that we can only be in harmony when everybody is on even ground.

The shame/grandiosity continuum

One thing that both shame and grandiosity have in common is that they require someone/something to measure against. Simply being alone probably won't induce shame until you compare yourself to a group of people having fun together. Being on a stage has no impact unless you have a cheering crowd to worship you. This commonality between grandiosity and shame can best be represented on a continuum, as follows:

Shame / Grandiosity Continuum

Shameful	Healthy Shame	Grandiose
"I am less than human"	"I am a human being"	"I am a God"
"I am inferior and incapable"	"I am capable & influential, with limits"	"I have infinite ability & power"
"I am not special"	"I am as worthy as the next person"	"I am better than everyone"
"I exist to serve others"	"We all exist to support each other"	"People exist to serve me"

Figure 3: *The shame/grandiosity continuum. Too much shame severely limits a person's life force and causes them to feel less than human, whereas too much grandiosity makes a person feel more than human and severely limits the life force of other people.*

When all people in a group are viewed as equal, they lie in the middle of the continuum and feel perfectly human. Recalling that every social hierarchy requires balance, the more grandiosity a person exhibits, the more shame other people are forced to experience in order to compensate. When grandiosity gets out of hand, it forces other people too far left on the continuum. The further left a person is pushed, the more inferior and unworthy they feel. Drifting too far to the right of the continuum causes a person to lose touch with their humanity and become more interested in their own well-being than that of others. They feel more than human. The middle of the continuum is a measure of healthy shame, where a person maintains a connection to their grandeur as well as their humanity.

In any relationship, the further right a person drifts on the continuum, the further left it forces the other person. By creating the impression that you have more or you are more, you are coercing the other person to experience their shame, whereas when two people are on equal terms, they both sit in the middle of the continuum and shame is effectively cancelled out.

The law of grandiosity

Grandeur is a strong and creative force. This overwhelming drive inside all of us to 'be more', while intoxicating, can lead to problems when it becomes grandiosity. As shown on the shame/grandiosity continuum, in any standard which we value, such as attractiveness or social status, somebody can usually convince us that they are above us. People of high status can set a bar and evoke our own shame response. Let's call this phenomenon the *law of grandiosity.*

The law of grandiosity is the shame-based reaction of a person who is met with someone who they perceive as being higher status.

This law dictates that we can react in five different ways:

- **Accept our low status:** We will be left to contend with our feeling of shame and will shrink ourselves so that balance is achieved on the continuum. This includes not rocking the boat and not making attempts to improve.
- **Attempt to meet the higher standard:** In this instance, shame acts as an agent for growth and improvement. For example, think of the men and women in the gym or at the salon, spurred on by the shameless beauty and health industry, which sets a benchmark of the perfect physical appearance.
- **Identify:** Some people choose to identify with a celebrity or sports figure. By following their every move and psychologically 'merging' themselves with the celebrity, a person effectively *becomes* the high-status figure. In doing so, they can completely sidestep their shame of being 'ordinary'. In their mind, they are up there with the star. They are on the same team as the high-status figure, and in doing so can live out their grandiosity instead of dwelling in shame.

- **Dis-identify:** Deeming a standard as unimportant will short-circuit the effect. Many people are not envious of celebrities and channel their grandeur instead; into their own art, for example. Someone's weight loss means nothing to you if you are not concerned with your own weight.
- **Attack:** Turning shame into rage is an attempt to reclaim power. Consider the snide remarks and put downs made in the comments section on social media. This is an attempt to shoot down the 'star' in order to counter the feeling of shame - i.e. the feeling of being below standard.

Shame is the reason we are so strongly affected by celebrities and other high-status social figures. Celebrities literally tower above us on billboards and movie screens. For many people, celebrities are difficult to ignore, since they are spoken about in all forms of media. They are marketed in such a way that they create the illusion of having more, knowing more and being more. In our social hierarchy, they are supposedly at the top.

The law of grandiosity and the shame/grandiosity continuum are not just limited to celebrities, however. They can apply equally to our friends and family who we perceive as higher status than us i.e. who we believe to have more assets, ability, wisdom or strength. They can apply in any relationship, romantic or otherwise, and they can definitely apply to the parent-child relationship.

The misunderstood emotion

As horrible as it can feel, shame is not actually there to harm us. It provides us with a feedback loop, reminding us not only when we are overdoing it, but also when we are not quite there. It serves a noble purpose. Knowing your limits allows you to function inside a more manageable structure. For example, before you can play a musical instrument, you need to learn your chords and theory first, followed by hundreds of hours of practice and a lot of trial and error. You need to face your limits and be reminded of them over and over again until you reach your goal. When another person outdoes you in something, your shame will inspire you to grow and to match the new standard. It stops one being complacent. In this context, shame is a useful tool.

The only way shame is harmful is when it is *irredeemable*. Not measuring up but having the chance to improve or change is life affirming, being placed in an endless loop of not being good enough is life crushing. There is great despair in feeling like you will *never* measure up. The hope of measuring up is how life spurs us into growth. That is life's intention; like two rugby teams, our grandeur should push up against our shame and maintain the pressure, claiming more and more ground, until it reaches the goal - or until we accept and make peace with our limitations.

Also, being equal and at one with others in your social circle feels great. It's the very essence of being human. By embracing our shame, we can live in a state of equality and humanity. We are psychologically godlike and physically mortal. We are *mortal gods*. We are all in this together. And we can only be aware of this through our shame.

When shame becomes toxic

Shame has a dark side. It doesn't always arise for good reason. It can be forced upon you by those who have no capacity for it. It can also be fabricated by those people looking to enhance their own sense of grandiosity. It really doesn't matter what the standard is, as long as you believe in it, you will be affected by it. The same goes the other way. If you look down on your friend's weaknesses, you might feel a sense of grandiosity. This can be used with deadly effect. If somebody creates a scenario where you believe that you are beneath them and makes you feel small, they will activate your shame. You will unwittingly dive into your dark, isolated, psychological purgatory, believing that you need to take inventory and improve. You will sink below the level of humanity and begin to feel less than human - you will feel inferior. If they shame you enough and reinforce it continuously in the relationship, you will stay there. It will become a part of your core identity. The result is *toxic shame*. You will cut yourself down to fit. You will lower your gaze, talk more quietly, express yourself less and doubt yourself more. You will become more cooperative and appeasing. Your respective places on opposite ends of the continuum will become solidified, and an unfair balance of power will be achieved.

This is exactly what the narcissist is counting on.

The core of the narcissist

To make us feel small in the right way is a function of art;
men can only make us feel small in the wrong way.

- E. M. Forster

The majority of humans are willingly influenced by their emotions. Some more than others. Empathy allows us to feel the plight of another person and want to help them. Shame regulates our grandiosity, and reminds us that we're not gods who need everyone to bow down to us, but rather that we are humans with flaws who need to get along and who are in need of constant improvement and adjustment. Guilt forces us to reflect on our wrong actions and make amends. These feelings can be painful, but they are also good. They help us maintain healthy relationships, to coexist and to create a better world.

Narcissists don't give a shit about any of that. They couldn't care less about your feelings. As far as they are concerned, feelings are not about creating a harmonious society or fostering fulfilling relationships - they are a way to control you. Gas-lighting, triangulation and hoovering are the subtle and often not so subtle techniques that narcissists use to control their targets through emotions. Saying a certain thing in a certain way can set off the emotions of their target and cause them to react. Narcissists are well aware of this. Tactics, however, crucial as they are to know, are focused on what the narcissist *does*. What we need to first understand, is what the narcissist *is*;

Narcissists are shameless.

This is the defining trait of narcissism. A narcissist is not in touch with their empathy or shame. Some people claim that narcissists have no capacity for shame at all, others that they have disowned their shame from an early age in exchange for a grandiose, false self. Either way, narcissists are shameless. Because they don't feel shame, their sense of grandiosity runs riot unchecked. In order to feel grandiose all the time, however, they need people to feed off. As a result, a narcissist lives out their grandiosity by subjugating and objectifying other people. On the shame/grandiosity continuum, the narcissist aims to push other people as far left as possible (shame), while maintaining their own position on the right (grandiosity).

Shamelessness is the most subtle thing about a narcissist and the most difficult to see. It is also at the core of a narcissist and what makes them so deadly to our well-being. By being shameless, the narcissist does not have to self-reflect. By being shameless, the narcissist does not have to admit to their limitations and humanity. It creates an impenetrable shield. They don't have to admit to being wrong, they don't have to admit to not being good enough, they don't have to apologise and they most definitely don't have to give others the higher ground.

Being in the presence of someone who is shameless automatically reflects all shame back onto you. By putting on an aura of godliness, it instantly causes the person in the narcissist's presence to feel inferior in comparison. When you are in the presence of a person who shows healthy shame, you feel warm and a sense of camaraderie and equality. When you are in the presence of a narcissist, more often than not, you feel like crap. Being raised by a narcissist or being in a relationship with a narcissist is like being under the hot sun all day. They reflect all shame back onto you just by being around you.

It can be easy to miss this if you spent an extended period of time in the presence of narcissists. They don't even have to do anything overtly abusive. It's not just about catching their manipulative behaviour, it's about being aware of how they make you feel. There's something off putting about it and it goes on just below your conscious awareness. It's like being in emotional purgatory. You are constantly waiting to be let in, to experience the joy of being in a satisfying, human relationship, but the narcissist keeps you at arms length. This is the core of a relationship with a narcissist; it all begins with this. They're like slippery fish. Nothing sticks to them. All flaws and shortcomings - i.e. anything human - get reflected back onto you. You are always the vulnerable one. By being shameless, the narcissist forces the other person to carry the shame – to feel inferior. As mentioned earlier, if the person feels it continuously and for long enough, they will eventually internalise it. It will become entwined with their personality and will exist as a constant shadow over a person's entire experience. Feeling anger for a long period of time makes a person become an angry person. Being depressed for a long period of time makes a person become a depressive person. Being exposed to shame for a long period of time makes a person believe that they are flawed to the bone. This toxic shame is what makes shamelessness in a relationship the most dangerous, even before any overt abuse takes place.

Shamelessness creates shame in others and is demonstrated in many subtle ways.

A narcissist might:

- **Strive always to be in control:** This can be as simple as impatiently snatching the broom from you when you're sweeping and doing the job themselves. Refusing to relinquish control or to allow a person to learn at their own pace makes them feel incapable of 'getting the job done'.

- **Use condescending stares/eye rolling:** A patronising look can communicate a message like "I'm doing you a favour just by tolerating you and allowing you to be around me".

- **Snicker and laugh at your weaknesses:** That all knowing laugh when you make a mistake communicates how amusing you are in comparison to a person who wouldn't make the same error. Quite often, the mistake is not even a mistake, but a snicker at something you simply did a different way to how the narcissist would do it. Not uncommon still is being laughed at even if you did something correctly, just to make you question yourself and think the narcissist knows something you don't.

- **Speak about you in the third person when you're present:** When you're discussed with someone else while present, especially in a non-favourable way, it can make you feel both shamed and powerless. For example, "Lisa has been so lazy around the house. She hasn't done any housework, she just watches Netflix all day." When this is said to someone else in your presence, it shines the light on you without actually including you in the conversation. It creates an illusion of two people of 'higher knowledge' discussing you: the object of 'concern'. Firstly, such a statement is subjective (Lisa might have felt a bit sick and watched Netflix for a few hours simply to unwind) and it forces you to either defend yourself or feel shame.

- **Inflate themselves through story:** Sharing stories which paint the narcissist in a highly superior way makes the listeners feel small in comparison. Many narcissists are great storytellers, and in their stories, they are usually strong and superior. An alternative way they boost their image in a story is not just by raising themselves up, but by putting down the person who they are describing in their story.

- **Inflate themselves through assertion and deflection:** A narcissist will avoid admitting weakness or to being limited. The narcissist might begin a sentence with "I never.." or "I always..". For example, "I never get dumped, I'm always doing the dumping" or "I always get through the queue within ten minutes". The second statement will come especially as a response to you saying that you had to wait for an hour. This separates them from the 'luckless fool', and makes them stand out as special.

- **Ask critical, rhetorical questions:** For example, "Why did you arrange the plates like that?" or "Why are you wearing those pants for?" These questions have no real answer or purpose other than to shine a light on your supposed incompetence.

- **Refuse to empathise and support:** When you share something genuine that's important to you, the narcissist will shut it down as quickly as possible or simply ignore it. They might simply nod, change the topic, or analyse and problem solve what you are saying. They do this so you cannot influence their emotions. This rejection of your genuine expression makes you feel shameful and unloved. Nothing is overtly done, yet it feels off when you realise that the person to whom you are opening your experience does not care enough to empathise.

- **Not allow you to set boundaries:** A narcissist might assume they know what's best for you - without consulting you first. They'll order your drink without asking, make decisions involving you without consulting, open your mail and so on. This objectifies you and makes you feel like the narcissist and only the narcissist knows what's best for you.

- **Refuse to go along with your plans or allow you to influence them:** The relationship is generally lopsided. They call the shots and decide where to go, what to do and for how long. They rely on the low self-esteem of their target to enforce this. Also, by not giving the target a preference, the narcissist can further erode the target's self-esteem.

- **Make unwelcome, supposedly neutral observations:** i.e. "You have hairs growing on your ears" or "You know, you're always the first to finish your food" or "You need to buy new shoes". This is designed to make you feel self-conscious without seeming like an actual attack.

- **Feign or exaggerate concern:** By exaggerating concern, the narcissist can make you feel like someone who needs help; even though you didn't feel that way to begin with. Although we do sometimes struggle in life, when concern is exaggerated, we can begin to feel like a basket case; i.e. someone who cannot cope with life. This fake or exaggerated concern normally comes with an accompanying look of worry.

- **Compare you to others:** When the narcissist points out that someone they know can do what you can't, or is better at something than you, they force you onto a scale of worth. Real or not, it is shaming and can be difficult to ignore. A man could be trying to put on weight at the gym, and then have his girlfriend point out how muscly her ex-boyfriend was. A parent can (subjectively) explain to their single daughter that every other woman her age is happily married and has children. These subtle comparisons undermine and shame.

Note that all of the above are designed to create the illusion that the target is of lower status and the narcissist is of higher status.

Comrades in shame

Those who find themselves on the left side of the shame/ grandiosity continuum for too long will internalise shame. They feel inferior and less than human. They feel like they don't deserve the support of others, but they themselves must provide it.

In a healthy relationship, on the other hand, the shame is shared and cancelled out. All parties work together to stay in the middle of the continuum. It is subconsciously communicated that we are both human, we both make mistakes and neither person is better than the other. We are equal. Whether it was intended or not, anything contrary to this, by definition, is shaming. For example, if a person explains to a friend that they embarrassed themselves showing off in front of someone attractive, the friend, as an act of acceptance and solidarity, might share a similar experience they had. Shame becomes a non-issue. If you share the same story with a narcissist, they might snicker and laugh at you and then talk about how attractive their last conquest was. In a healthy relationship, what you share is respected and given importance by the other person. Your boundaries are respected, and the relationship is about sharing and equality, not control and competition. There are no mind games. You laugh together with the other person, not be the target of their ridicule.

Those with healthy shame and empathy will:

- Mirror back your emotions
- Look for ways to laugh *with* you
- Admit to being wrong without making excuses
- Give you the space to express yourself
- Tailor their emotional experience to ensure a connection is achieved with you
- Be comfortable having boundaries in the relationship
- Allow for equal status in the relationship
- Respect your vulnerability and allow themselves, in turn, to be vulnerable

When a person has people around them who work for equality and a balanced standing on the shame/grandiosity continuum, they will have *healthy shame*. They believe in their potential and self-worth, but accept their own limitations and respect the rights of others to express their own grandeur. They are not defined by their shame, nor do they allow it to control them. They simply use it for growth and to get along well with those they care about. They seek ways to thrive while also co-existing with and supporting others. They most definitely do not tolerate shamelessness in others.

Responding to shamelessness

As stated earlier, the law of grandiosity encourages one of five shame-based reactions. This law can also be applied to narcissism. When in a relationship with a narcissist, the target can react to shamelessness as follows:

- **Accept their low status:** Toxic shame will run riot. If the narcissist is a parent, the child will have no choice but to accept their position in the pecking order. As an adult, if the narcissist has sufficiently broken the target's self-esteem or has sucked the target into a relationship with them, the target will be cajoled into accepting their low status.
- **Attempt to live up to the narcissist's standards:** The target could try harder to please, or to explain and defend themselves, or to make changes and improvements. The narcissist will simply raise the bar.

This never ends and almost always leads to an overwhelming feeling of shame.

- **Identify with the narcissist:** This is the most common. For a child, identifying with the parent and viewing them as omnipotent and good is automatic. It's a necessary survival tactic. In a relationship with a narcissist, the target will be convinced that they are in a loving, equal partnership. Many people simply care for those they are close to, and so their love keeps them positively identified with the narcissist and everything that comes along with that.

- **Dis-identify from the narcissist:** Children do not have this option. In adulthood, this is usually the best path to take. It can involve ending the relationship or withdrawing emotional involvement as a protection mechanism. This will be explained in more detail later, in the chapter titled 'Scorched Earth'.

- **Discredit the narcissist:** Slugging it out with a narcissist is not recommended. They are well trained in and thrive on mind games. Sinking to their level will only serve to give them narcissistic supply. This will also be explored in more detail later.

The core of the target

Redemption is not perfection. The redeemed must realise their imperfections.

- John Piper

On the true self

At the core of every person is the true self. This true self is emotion, creativity, spontaneity, energy, curiosity, love, peace, intuition and of course; grandeur. It doesn't know logic, and it doesn't have eyes in the world; it leaves that to the thinking mind. Instead, the true self can sense the world in ways the mind cannot. The mind has the ability to learn, store, process and use the information given to it. The true self has the capacity to *generate* new knowledge from thin air. Where the mind *analyses* and *compares,* the true self *intuits* and *feels,* and through that feeling, integrates the world around it into its core. It's a very sensitive part of us, and without protection, can be damaged and negatively affected in countless ways. We've all seen the wonder and vigour of a child. This is the child's true self on display;

before their mind develops fully and begins to filter their experience.

Being connected with your true self creates an abundance of energy and inspiration. Although it is sensitive, it's also the most powerful part of us. It's our life force. When integrated, it gives us access to our humanity as well as our creative power. It connects all human beings. Although the mind can rehash many facts, the true self can empathise with another person and help us build a connection. Facts can only take us so far. It's the intuitive power of the true self which makes us effective as human beings and allows us to live up to our potential. Your true self is numinous; having it there all the time is like having a good friend at your side as you take on life's challenges. It is life itself acting through us. It's adaptable and evolutionary.

This true self can be disowned. Humans have a natural need to be seen, understood, respected and loved. When these four needs are met, the true self thrives. The person feels integrated, whole and has a sense of direction. When a person is shamed without redemption, they become stagnant, powerless, and fragmented, and their self-esteem drops. The strength of your relationship with your true self and your self-esteem are directly correlated.

For the true self to thrive, we need resonance from the world. We need those around us to understand, accept and support our current state. Resonance means being allowed to express our emotions, good or bad. If we express sadness about something, the other person may reject our expression with a backhanded 'Just cheer up, everything will be fine'. If, on the other hand, the other person relates to and feels our sadness, then resonance is achieved, which is two people sharing an emotional state or 'mood', regardless of what it is. It is two people connected through their feelings.

The more resonance we receive, the stronger our life force becomes and the more momentum the true self has. Can you think back to times when you felt supported and loved, and as a result, you felt incredibly energetic and excited to embrace life? This doesn't just come from romantic relationships, but from any figure in our lives who truly understands us. Love and support are life affirming. It makes our world go round. Being shamed and having your core self rejected or attacked, on the other hand, puts a halt to this process. The beauty of the true self is instead doused with doubt and subjected to strict and critical introspection. When excessively shamed, the true self is analysed, questioned, judged and then ultimately rejected.

On the ego

The ego is based in the mind. It's our representative in the world; a collection of thoughts, beliefs and ideas about how the world is and how we should interact with it. It also holds the idea of who we are in the world. That is, it controls how we relate to people and what elements of our personality we show to (or hide from) others. Intuition, energy and love are what truly make us human, but we still need to know how to pay our bills, read maps, follow social norms, communicate and of course, understand when we are being manipulated.

On the false self

The false self is a construct of the ego. It is a repertoire of behaviours which make up a personality. What makes it 'false' is that it's not based on the true self. It doesn't take its cues from a person's emotions. Recall that the true self needs safety, love, respect and understanding to thrive. For the target, when genuine emotional connection does not exist, or worse, when they are being abused, it can be extremely painful to experience the true self. For the narcissist, experiencing the true self means experiencing their shame. The solution for either situation is to create a false self which can take over and act on behalf of the true self, manipulating reality to make it more bearable.

The false self serves two purposes:

- It keeps a person from directly experiencing their true self and therefore from being influenced by the outside world, which in turn reduces the amount of shame and pain felt.
- It allows a person to manipulate their environment in the hope of getting their needs met.

Both narcissists and targets have a false self. It is a prerequisite for the target to have one before they can actually interact with a narcissist. In the case of the narcissist, their intended use of the false self is to dominate others, which they hope can achieve them control and garner them narcissistic supply. In the case of the target, they use the false self to keep them from being abandoned.

Over their lifetime, the narcissist creates a set of behaviours which combine potently to form their false self. This creates a fog screen which keeps people from reaching the narcissist's true self. The narcissist's false self is usually very compelling to the uninitiated. It takes a while to realise that you're not dealing directly with a real person. The narcissist is extremely skilled at distracting you from ever seeing through it.

Some basic examples of a false self which narcissists create are:

- **The Storyteller:** Tells story after story, painting themselves as the person in power. They also tell victim stories, but then explain how they overcame the situation and gained the upper hand.
- **The Victim:** Things never go right for them. They feed people stories of their misfortune and then reject any suggestions for fixing the situation. Their only intention is to keep others emotionally invested in their problems for as long as possible.
- **The Strong Silent Type:** Shows no emotion, excitement or weakness. They have a stoic demeanour and invest little in their relationships. This gives them an air of superiority in the eyes of their target.
- **The Clown:** Makes light of every situation, makes witty remarks that put down what other people say, plays pranks and sucks up your attention by showing you funny videos online.
- **The Intellectual:** Uses monologues as a way to entrap another person or even a group of people, sucking up the energy and the focus of a group with their words.

- **The Matriarch/Patriarch:** The parent or the manager traditionally play this role. They use their position as an excuse to act shameless while coercing the child or the employee to worship them and subject themselves to them.

All of the above roles are tools for control. Which tool gets used depends on the narcissist but also on the power and self-esteem of their target. For example, the narcissist will enforce their matriarch/patriarch role on their child, who has minimal power, barking orders and ridiculing them, then switch to playing the victim with their empathic sister and then play storyteller or clown with their friend. If a friend has low self-esteem, then the matriarch/patriarch role can still be used. They will simply probe until they find a way to control their target. To the narcissist, it doesn't matter *how* they control their target, as long as they can achieve it. If they cannot manipulate their target overtly, then having the target's attention is control enough for them. As long as it's under their terms, the narcissist is getting their narcissistic supply.

When interacting with the false self of a narcissist, it's like watching a stage show or reading a novel. The act is elaborate and compelling. It's intended to draw you in on the narcissist's terms and keep you under their influence.

They never break character. The narcissist's false self is both compelling and absolute. Once you're drawn in, you stay there. There is no going any further. It's all head and no heart, and feels somehow empty and leaves you with a sense of despair. A lot is said and done, but deep down no genuine connection is achieved, and no growth is experienced. It's like binge watching television or being trapped in a washing machine cycle that never ends.

Looking in the wrong place

To some degree, we all have a false self. It's a handy tool for negotiating with the world. Eventually, we take it off like a business suit and revert to a more genuine, feeling based dialogue with our loved ones. Narcissists, however, have their false self on 24/7 and use it on everyone, no matter how close that person is to them. Their intention is to control, not to experience genuine connection and internal growth. Vulnerability for them is a no-go zone. As a result, they cannot offer resonance since they aren't in touch with their feelings. Furthermore, the narcissist has a very specific reality which must be enforced; their target must stay fixated and orbit them like a star. When in a relationship with a narcissist, the target is clearly not accepted for who they are, no matter how badly they need it. Instead, they are cornered into playing a specific role which helps bolster the narcissist's grandiosity. To achieve acceptance, the target works on creating their own false self which is compatible with that of the narcissist. This false self is a set of behaviours put on by the target in the hope of avoiding abandonment, since showing their true self is clearly a cause for rejection.

The most common role is the nice person persona. When playing this role, the target is extremely well behaved and cooperative. This kind of persona tends to be reinforced and rewarded by the narcissist, for obvious reasons. Even if the target is angry, or frustrated, or feels hurt, they will have to keep playing nice because they cannot threaten the narcissist's strict arrangement. This is what makes such a self false. It's not congruent with how the target really feels and what they really need in the current moment. Rather than identifying and connecting with their true self, the target identifies with a construct in their mind, which is conditioned by the narcissist. Through this conditioning, they *become* a strict set of behaviours and beliefs.

The target is coerced into mirroring the narcissist as follows:

- **The Storyteller:** The target becomes a good listener, and can only contribute to the relationship by telling stories of their own. The most despairing part is that every story the target tells will be topped by the narcissist. It becomes a competition which the narcissist must always win.
- **The Victim:** The target adapts by investing their emotions into the narcissist's endless problems. If the target tries to express their own misfortune, the narcissist switches off.
- **The Strong Silent Type:** The target invests the emotion and vulnerability into the relationship, and relies on the narcissist to be predictable and a person of strength. The target feels both reassured and frustrated by the narcissist's rigidity.
- **The Clown:** The target becomes a willing audience to the narcissist, laughing at or even being the butt of their jokes.
- **The Incessant Talker:** The target listens with a feeling of despair, unable to break out. The imbalance takes its toll over time and shame arises.
- **The Matriarch/Patriarch:** The target will be infantilised. All decisions are made by the narcissist, and the target is not given a voice. The target is only recognised when they behave as the narcissist expects them to.

When relating in such a way, the target is fooled into believing they have succeeded in securing the narcissist's love. However, the narcissist is only in love with their own false self. Love is impossible, since effectively what the target has is a false self 'relating' to the false self of the narcissist, who cares only for their own self image. The emotional distance here is obvious.

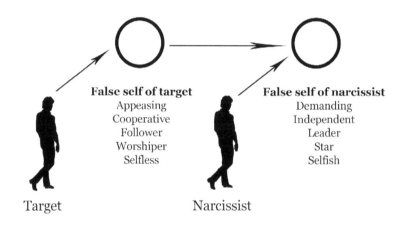

Figure 4: *The interplay between a narcissist and a target. The narcissist is identified with a false self image. The target in turn identifies with their own false self image, which worships the false self image of the narcissist. True connection is impossible.*

This arrangement keeps the target from being abandoned by the narcissist but does not cater to their needs.

Something further must be done. The true self will not be denied. It craves connection and an outlet for its grandeur. The result is *dissociation*.

Goodbye world

Having a false self worshipping another false self is a lonely experience. The true self of the target feels neglected and, as a result, shameful. The target tries seeking the approval of the narcissist but is met with emotional distance, shaming, distractive behaviour and, when the narcissist deems it necessary, rage. The narcissist abhors the target's needs. Hence the target's sense of grandeur is given no outlet to express itself. The target needs desperately to stop feeling the pain of loneliness, shame and neglect. If they don't have anybody in their life to offer them resonance, they resort to dissociation, viewing the world and themselves through their imagination instead. In doing so, they gain an outlet for their true self and control over their self image.

Just like the narcissist, this imagined self is omnipotent in comparison to the real, shame-based true self. By this definition, the target is also being narcissistic, since they are rejecting their humanity and identifying with a self that's flawless. The key difference, however, is how they go about it. The narcissist expresses their grandiosity by *engaging* the world, albeit by subjecting, objectifying and controlling others. The target of a narcissist will instead *disengage* from the world and dwell in fantasy i.e. their grandiose self exists in their imagination.

Living in dissociation is a coping mechanism, which creates a new reality, away from the true self, away from the real world and away from the painful experience of toxic shame. When a narcissist is forced to face their shame, their tactic is to lie, deflect, manipulate and, if necessary, react with rage. In the case of a target, they simply drift away into their safe fantasy world. In this fantasy world, the target can be anybody they want to be. They are never less than anybody, they are never put down, and they do not have to feel the friction of the real world. When dissociated, the target loses touch with their thinking mind and their true self; they go somewhere else entirely. In their imagination, they can snatch back power and love. They can win that argument with the narcissist and feel a sense of power. They can conjure up resonance, imagining interactions where people hear them and understand them, and with that feel a sense of love. The imagination becomes a tool of release for the very real needs of the true self.

An integrated ego

In an ideal world, a person in the early stages of life is led by the hand through the jarring experience of being human. As they start to feel their emotions and begin to get a sense of their true self, they are met with internal limits and external obstacles with which they are taught strategies to find their way through. Shame is felt as a mild pressure, but it doesn't overwhelm the person, and the person doesn't lose heart. Emotions will generally not overwhelm; the person is taught to manage them, step by step, as they come up. The person continues to feel their internal strength and grandeur regardless. Their expressions of emotion, good or bad, are mostly accepted by their loved ones. There is no role to be played. Further to this, the primary figures in their life will adapt and occasionally manipulate reality, not to make the person feel less than, but to make them feel special and equal. When this balance is reached, a person feels special and human, all at the same time. On the shame/grandiosity continuum, they are somewhere in the middle. Their journey through life is a flat field, where obstacles can be managed, and support is at hand. The result of such an upbringing is a well-trained ego. The person is conscious of all of their emotions. They can identify them, withstand them and then make the right choices. They have high self-esteem and are socially confident, rather than socially anxious. The true self is integrated. The mind becomes aware of social norms and behaviours, and can accommodate the emotional world of the true self when making decisions, as well as the emotional world of others. When emotions become overwhelming, the person has resources for self-care and feels worthy enough to ask for help. They understand themselves enough to know what kind of help they need. They become well versed on mediating between their true self and the world. A *healthy* ego is created.

The word ego is typically associated with narcissism, in that whoever has an ego is stuck-up and self-absorbed. In fact, the definition of ego in psychology is *"the part of the mind that mediates between the conscious and the unconscious and is responsible for reality testing and a sense of personal identity"*.

A healthy ego is a mediator, making logical decisions based on what it sees in the world and what the true self is telling it. It is the eyes of our true self. It's also a construct of the mind - it's not real. Zen Buddhism describes the ego as an obstacle to knowing your true self. This can be true, since a false self can cut a person off from their core experience. But the ego is also necessary for navigating the world. The ego is the gatekeeper who decides what is good and what is bad for the true self.

The consequences of dissociation

For the target of narcissism, life is a treacherous, never-ending climb and support is simply not there. When engaging the world, they crash and burn, over and over again. Their emotions are overwhelming, and they feel like they are constantly under attack. They don't have a safe space to develop their healthy ego. They search frantically for a way out until they discover that magical place in their mind, above the clouds, where there's no turbulence and where they don't have to deal with the pain and friction of daily life.

This dissociated state has many dire consequences, however:

- **Stunted learning:** We learn about the world when we feel safe. Our emotions are managed, and we can focus enough to absorb whatever concepts we need for our daily life. From a dissociated state, however, facts are overlooked. Important concepts are glossed over and become abstractions. The details aren't filled in. For example, a person viewing the world from a dissociated state will talk about that street they visited, with all those trees. A well-trained ego will know the name of the street, where it was located, that it is popular with tourists, remember some of the stores and vividly recall how it felt to be there. With a healthy ego, knowledge and experience are integrated.

- **Inability to handle feelings:** When forced to engage with the world, the target is also forced to engage their emotions. Living in fantasy means the target has little practice in understanding and processing their feelings. Managing your life requires a strong, well-trained ego, which sets limits and boundaries so that emotions can roam without getting out of hand. For example, a well-trained ego will know that a certain friend, while fun, is also emotionally exhausting to spend time with, and will make a decision to either limit time spent or limit the topics discussed so that energy is conserved. A well-trained ego will support a friend in need, then know when to have alone time to recharge. In a dissociated state, a person will hardly be aware of why they are exhausted.

- **Deferred control:** A person must be engaged with the world to have control over their life. But targets are not engaged and will leave a lot of their life decisions up to other people; people who are more engaged and supposedly know better. They will relinquish control to a narcissist.

- **Susceptibility to manipulation:** This deferral of control leaves a target open to manipulation. Because the target doesn't have a well-informed ego to mediate and set boundaries, the narcissist gets easy access to manipulate.
- **Poor memory:** A person who dissociates will have gaps in their memory. It's not uncommon for children of narcissism to forget the details of most of their childhood. They can be forgetful in general.
- **Increased anxiety:** Trying to maintain a perfect world is difficult because the target *has* to interact with the imperfect environment around them. Social anxiety is common, since exposing oneself to others means having to face your true self and be engaged. This shatters the illusion and brings the true self screaming into the real world like a baby snatched from the womb. The target is not accustomed to exposing their true self to the world. The narcissist made sure of that.
- **Alienation from self:** When dissociated, nobody is home to take care of things. Emotional needs are ignored, anxiety runs rampant, and self-development and growth is stunted since the person is not in touch with their true self and its wants and needs. It is a very lonely experience.
- **Weak relationships:** Being friends or in a relationship with someone who dissociates is difficult, for obvious reasons. A relationship needs engagement, intimacy, integrity and strength. To remain dissociated requires a

rigid environment, where nothing is too challenging. Life by nature is challenging, and this flows into relationships. Others need to sense a person has a backbone. When dissociated, long term relationships are usually based on a set of rigid roles and behaviours, rather than genuine emotion and flexibility.

The target, while dissociated, lives in constant fear. This will continue until they become conscious of the fact and then create a safe, nurturing environment that allows them to come out of hiding. The process of dropping the fantasy and re-entering the world is a jarring and difficult process, but nonetheless a journey which the target will have to take as they establish a life outside of the narcissist regime.

The solution to dissociation involves a safe environment, resonance from others, dissolving the false self i.e. identifying which submissive behaviours were created due to fear of abandonment, and simultaneously integrating the true self into the ego i.e. becoming self-reliant and learning to cater to the needs of the true self. This process will be explored later when the seven practices are introduced.

The game

We can look at human interaction as a sport in which we all engage. Each of us gets to put on a mask, and depending on the situation, we enact a set of back and forth behaviours which provide a structure for relating to another human being. And just like in sport, there are rules and expectations. For example, how we structure formal emails, how we greet each other and the topics we avoid discussing.

The position of the person will affect how we interact with them. How we treat our doctor, for example, is unique. We speak carefully, and we look up to them for answers, as we would an oracle. The plaque on the door determines the rules of engagement. In turn, the doctor is expected to behave professionally and provide us with a service. In these cases, the framework which holds us together is pre-determined. The workplace, the doctor's office, the police uniform and so on. Clearly, any person can abuse their position, but there is at least a framework within which they are expected to behave.

In personal relationships, no formal framework exists. We are bound to each other by choice, and the boundaries are not explicitly set from outside. The game is governed by something much deeper and much more personal: *our emotions*. And with that we become far more vulnerable. The relationship is the playing field and emotions are how we play. When somebody oversteps our boundaries, our anger might be how we alert them. When we feel that somebody is threatening our relationship, a feeling of jealousy can spur us to speak to our partner. If we do wrong by another person and hurt them, our guilt challenges us to make amends.

Effectively, we engage in the game of human relations when we engage our emotions. The more emotionally invested we are in a person, the more likely we are to listen to them and they to us. We give each other our time, and we allow ourselves to be influenced by the other person in various ways. Through our emotions, a person stops being an object and starts being a human being who we love and whose well-being we find important. The relationship exists internally in our hearts and minds. Another person is allowed real estate in our most intimate places. They are allowed access to our true self, the place beyond the mind and behind our social mask. As the relationship develops, we become more and more attached to the person. This attachment is a bond, which is very real, and emotion is what holds it together. By opening up our true self to a person, we are opening ourselves to be emotionally influenced - and of course, manipulated. The one fundamental, unspoken rule of the game is the golden rule, which is to treat others as you would like to be treated. That is, as members of one society, we are all affected by our emotions, and as a result, we need to treat each other's boundaries with respect and be careful not to push each other's buttons.

Narcissists are well aware of the golden rule and how most people play by it. They function under its protection yet will not hesitate to break it. They also know how emotions work. They know that we allow ourselves to open up when we like someone. They know that if they can make you feel small or inferior, that you will be washed over with shame. They are aware that if they play the victim, your guilt will kick in and you will work hard to rectify the situation. They know if they mirror you in the right way, you will start to like them, and that if they tell you a heartfelt story, you will empathise and they will endear themselves to you. They know that if they charm you well enough and play their cards right, you will grow attached to them. The narcissist also knows how you will react when they threaten that attachment. They are aware of how overwhelming emotions can be, and how big a part emotions play in the game. They also know that it doesn't matter if the situations are fabricated; the emotional reaction will still apply.

The thing is, they don't respond the same way we do. They don't feel shame or guilt, and their emotions don't influence them like they do other people. As a result, they can bombard the target's emotional circuits without remorse; distracting the target from the truth, wearing down their self-esteem and keeping them second-guessing themselves. The narcissist is well-versed in the game of human relations, and is skilled at influence. Without their conscience to keep them in line, they become proficient manipulators. In addition to this, they are more than willing to combine manipulation with social frameworks for double effect. They are well aware of the increased power that comes if they enter politics. They thrive as the manager in the office, which gives them a license to tell others what to do. It's no surprise that narcissists typically gravitate to positions of power. Yet even if they don't have a social framework to assist them, they know that if they create the *illusion* of being higher status, they can use the law of grandiosity to their advantage. They constantly look for ways to create and enforce a hierarchy where they are on top, using shame as their primary weapon. They see the emotions of others as a tool and the game of human relationships as a sport which must be engaged in and won while showing no regard for the golden rule. They stare at their target with their wide open eyes and dilated pupils knowing full well that the game is on, and they are going to win.

Step into my web: Mind Control 101

If you don't control your mind, someone else will.

- John Allston

Narcissists want the target under their control. Before having this, however, the narcissist will need to draw the target into their sphere of influence. They achieve this in a multitude of ways, with the two most common being *sanctioned superiority* and *charm*.

Sanctioned Superiority

If the narcissist is a parent or in management, then their task becomes much easier. When in a natural position of power, the narcissist is seen by the target as both superior and as a source of structure and guidance. Having sanctioned control over another human being is extremely helpful for the narcissist; it's the easiest way to get free supply. Many parents unwittingly do this, keeping their children trapped in a cage of guilt and manipulation so that they don't stray too far away from them. It's important to note that such parents don't all have narcissistic personality disorder, but this tendency in a parent is narcissistic.

Further to their sanctioned position of power, the narcissist will assert their dominance by ridiculing and shaming those beneath them and acting shameless. This strategy helps add to the aura that the narcissist is of higher status. By keeping the target washed over with shame, the target becomes more compliant. Recall that shame is the equaliser emotion, which encourages us to behave how society expects in order to be accepted.

As a child grows, and depending on how much healthy shame their parent shows, they will tone down their god-like perception of the parent and begin to see them for what they are; human beings with flaws. This natural transition becomes thwarted, however, if the parent is a narcissist. Their shamelessness and grandiosity mixed with a child's impressionability is a dangerous cocktail. Society compounds this by making it taboo to question the person who brought you into this world. Therefore, seeing your parents or family members in any negative light brings about intense feelings of guilt.

It can also be tough to see your manager as feeding off you for narcissistic supply since you expect to take orders from somebody who is above you in the work hierarchy. The working relationship is not the measure of narcissism, however. It is the attitude toward and the treatment of others which makes the difference. To the narcissist, an employee is an object who will do what they are told and give the narcissist their supply. To a person of healthy shame, an employee is a person with basic rights who has agreed to take on a role in exchange for a salary.

A narcissistic manager will:

- Expect their employee to work overtime with no regard for the employee's stress levels or overall happiness
- Put down the employee and prey on their weaknesses
- Blur the lines when it comes to contractual obligations and manipulate their employee into going above the call of duty
- Enforce one-way communication, not allowing the employee to question them or their agenda
- Make verbal and personal attacks against the employee
- Instigate drama and confusion when communicating with their employees

A manager with healthy shame will instead:

- Encourage a high level of work while respecting the happiness and well-being of their employee
- Enforce the manager-employee relationship while respecting the basic rights of the employee
- Rely on a feedback loop with the employee and hold themselves accountable to ensure the working relationship is healthy
- Respect the employee's rights to personal boundaries

To summarise, a position of superiority and a shameless attitude are a potent combination, especially against those who have grown accustomed to life under a narcissist regime.

Charm

Charm is useful in the absence of power hierarchies, used to lure the target into the narcissist's sphere of influence.

When using charm, the narcissist communicates two things to their targets; *I like you,* and *I am just like you.* When you meet a normal person, they usually show a healthy scepticism of you, and it takes time to build their trust. If you have enough in common with each other, you will bond slowly over those similarities. You build trust between each other in a gradual and steady fashion. Most often, though, the similarities are not strong enough, and what little of the relationship you have formed effectively dies off.

With a narcissist, the relationship hits the ground running. The narcissist apparently shares many of the things that you enjoy. They are very engaging and quick to do you small favours which you haven't requested. They make most of your relationships look bland in comparison. The more impressionable you are to charm, the more likely the narcissist will use it.

Some signs that the narcissist is using charm on you are:

- They actually say "I like you" very soon after meeting you.
- They make intense, unflinching eye contact.
- They act very agreeable and nice, but might suddenly switch focus and pretend like you don't even exist.
- They share a lot of your interests, but only through conversation. There's no actual proof of it.
- They offer you their undivided attention and contact you consistently (Also known as Love Bombing).

You can also tell if a narcissist is using charm by your gut feeling. Normally it feels good and off-putting at the same time. Like a robot trying to imitate human emotions, there is a machine-like feel about it, mainly because they are putting it on - it's not real. A person with healthy shame and good intentions will be uncomfortable with too much eye contact, will not be interested in you without strong reasons and will be able to demonstrate clearly that they share your interests.

If a target is between relationships or feels starved of love, then any attention will be welcomed. The target will have no choice; the pull will be magnetic and almost irresistible. It won't feel right, but their need for attention and acceptance will override their gut instinct. This early stage in a relationship is crucial for the narcissist. Once they can establish rapport and get their target to invest, then manipulating the target becomes much easier. We are much more agreeable with people who we like.

The charm will stay on until one or both of the following happens:

- **The target is completely won over:** Once the narcissist has the target completely invested in the relationship, the charm can be turned off. At this stage, the target has been disarmed and has let go of any scepticism. If control over the target starts slipping, then charm can be switched on again.

- **The target is no longer useful to the narcissist:** This cycle can happen over and over again, where the narcissist will charm their way into the target's affections, get whatever they need (an ego boost, a favour, company) and then switch it off again. It can also happen in romantic relationships, where the narcissist either begins acting more distant and secretive or leaves the relationship altogether without notice.

The key way to know when the narcissist is using charm is that it can be switched on and off. Lavish and enthusiastic praise becomes radio silence. Then when the target begins to let go or the narcissist needs some fresh supply, it comes on again full power. This merry-go-round can happen in a relationship or with an acquaintance. It depends on what the narcissist needs at that moment. Normally the reasons for a person's disengagement are there, like stress or being overwhelmed. It's noticeable, or they could even remain engaged on a lower level and explain their situation. With a narcissist, it will simply switch off as though the warmth that the target thought was there never existed. It is *sudden* and *swift*, and can often be the only red flag you will notice. The narcissist will simply leave a phone text unanswered or just stare, eyes glazed over, with little regard for the target.

Using sanctioned superiority or charm, the narcissist has pulled the target under their sphere of influence. The next step will be to cement their control. They achieve this by breaking down and then recreating the target's identity as well as reprogramming their reality.

Hijacking your reality

If somebody spotted a mole on your hand, and then with a look of shock and concern told you that you're gravely ill and that you should immediately go to the hospital, would you believe them? Probably not. You know a mole is a sunspot, and that when it's brown, it's harmless. You have confidence in your ability to read reality.

What if somebody told you that you had something in your hair? Would you believe them? Probably, but by checking with your hands or with a mirror you could easily verify the truth.

What if somebody, instead, told you something that was open to interpretation? What if they said that your hair looks funny today? Or that you look grumpy all the time? That not many people like you? Maybe that you dress oddly? Or that you're inconsiderate?

A person who respects the golden rule and who has a moral compass knows the power of words, and would carefully consider their statements, opinions and judgements before sharing them. They will test them for truth and consider their impact on people. A narcissist, on the other hand, will make judgements and say hurtful things which target a person's insecurities - without hesitation - and act as though they are gospel.

Often it's not what you say, but how you say it. The narcissist will say things with such conviction and passion that the person hearing it will be strongly inclined to believe it. The narcissist will rely on this conviction and the weaknesses of their target to further their agenda.

While a narcissist is charming their way into your heart, they are simultaneously fishing for insecurities. Once they discover those weaknesses, they can use them as entry points into your mind. Your deepest insecurities mostly come from childhood. When they are brought up, especially by someone close to you, they reopen those wounds and make you even more vulnerable. Supposedly innocent remarks engage your emotions and open up small gaps which allow the narcissist into your most sensitive spaces.

Subjective remarks are a potent weapon in the war for your mind. The aim is to break down your sense of reality and then create a new one, where you are a pawn in the narcissist's game.

This hijacking process is carried out by the narcissist in three steps:

1. They break down your identity: They might question how you arranged the books on the shelf or tell you that the way you did your hair looks odd. They tell you that you put on weight recently. They tell you that you don't spend enough time with them and that even their ex, who they described as selfish and incompetent, gave them more time than you did. They tell you that your friends are rude and stuck up. You're too emotional or even too emotionally distant. You need to focus more on your career and earn more money. You're self-centred and don't care enough about the feelings of others. It is these subtle and often unsubstantiated opinions and remarks which wear down a person and make them believe that they are incompetent compared to the narcissist. They are designed to make you question yourself and your reality. It won't be uncommon to feel a sense of shame and unworthiness for days after spending time with a narcissist. You start asking yourself;

am I getting fat? Am I too self-centred? It's only a matter of time before these persistent, subtle attacks break through.

2. They begin feeding you a new identity: As the narcissist breaks down your self-esteem and your identity, shame runs riot. The more washed over with shame you become, the more you will scramble to redeem yourself. The time is then ripe to begin feeding you a new identity, which will naturally involve you being whatever the narcissist needs you to be. By telling you that you're being too emotional or giving you a distasteful look when you express your emotions, they cause you to compensate by showing less emotion, all with the aim of stunting your ability to express yourself in the relationship. By telling you that you're self-centred, they cause you to compensate for this false standard by giving them more and more of your attention. By laughing at your choice of clothing, they cause you to express less of your individuality and instead come deeper into their web, even going as far as to dress how they expect you to. By consistently ridiculing and attacking your friends and family, they cause you to question your relationships, and in turn slowly but surely disengage from the people in your life and invest more in your relationship with the narcissist. The narcissist does not want you to have a network to rely on; they want you dependent entirely on them, where they can have you under their control.

3. They use a reward/punish strategy to finalise the new identity: If you behave how the narcissist expects, they will usually reward you with compliments, attention or sex. If your original identity comes through, or you do not act as expected, they will punish you by verbally attacking you, resuming their attack on your identity, expressing their distaste, ridiculing and shaming you or giving you the cold shoulder.

The narcissist makes you believe things that aren't true. When you have a warped sense of reality, you won't have any idea how to feel or act. Their twisted manipulations then become your reality. They have control over your mind. All you know is that you keep messing up, and they don't. So you conclude that the narcissist is much more competent and powerful than you. Your self-esteem drops more and more, and your new identity as the underling takes over.

Understand your obstacles

If you're trying to achieve, there will be roadblocks. I've had them; everybody has had them. But obstacles don't have to stop you. If you run into a wall, don't turn around and give up. Figure out how to climb it, go through it, or work around it.

- Michael Jordan

You've got an understanding of grandiosity and shame and how it can bind you to the narcissist. You've learnt about the destructive effects of toxic shame. You know how the narcissist uses the false self to simultaneously achieve control and emotional distance. You know how the rules of human engagement are manipulated and broken by the narcissist and you have a basic idea of how mind control works. You're amped up for action. But before you dive in, it helps to understand the obstacles you will face as you fight this battle.

Obstacle one: Enmeshment

Being kept in an enmeshed, submissive state means your sense of self depends on the narcissist. Without a strong, individual identity, your willpower and self-esteem are compromised. This makes it more difficult to act in your best interest.

Although you are not to blame, you will be an unwilling part of the problem. The fight will rage on inside you. Having your sense of self hijacked and your internal strength compromised weakens your willpower.

Your psychological state will work against you and fight you as you try to change, or worse, you'll unconsciously replay the same dynamics over and over again. Like a fish in water, it can be hard to tell what life is like not being under the hypnotic spell of a narcissist. It takes vigilance, conscious effort and courage to turn the tide.

Obstacle two: The psychological cage

The narcissist regime limits the target's reality down to a specific role. The longer the target lives under this regime, the more they internalise it. The mind absorbs its environment and adapts to it. The reality which the narcissist creates becomes that of the target. This reality is effectively a cage which keeps the target imprisoned. Internalising this cage turns it into a *psychological cage*. The target lives their life with the belief that they cannot go any further than a certain set of limits. Even if they escape the narcissistic abuse, the target will continue to live within their psychological cage.

Stepping outside of the cage induces anxiety and fear. The target is institutionalised. It's crucial to be aware of this concept since it can function without being seen. Do you feel silly trying new things? Does the opinion of others keep you from rocking the boat? Do you feel extreme fear and anxiety when you are made responsible for something? Does the unknown frighten the hell out of you? This can be the psychological cage in action. The psychological cage is a very real thing, along with the fear that comes about whenever a situation threatens it.

Obstacle three: Love starvation

At our core, we have an inherent, insatiable need to be seen, heard, respected and understood. If you were raised by or spent considerable time with a narcissist, you were most likely starved of this. Even after you've physically freed yourself, it takes consistent, attuned care to satisfy that hunger and return you to emotional equilibrium. You can't just shut it off. Narcissists see this hunger from a long way away and will use it to manipulate you. It's like a gravitational force which acts against your will and clouds your judgement, which might lead you to make the wrong choices unwittingly.

Obstacle four: Low shame tolerance

To live well, it's crucial that you have a tolerance for shame. Being dissociated from the true self means being disconnected from shame. The problem is that anytime a target is forced to face their limits, or anytime they make a mistake, intense shame comes up, forcing the target to dissociate again and dwell in their imagination. Rather than be a firm pressure which they can push against for feedback, it becomes a frightening beast which must be avoided at all costs. The problem is that you cannot make changes or grow unless you are consistently in touch with your shame. You need to be engaged with life, making mistakes and adjusting course continuously. If you are reluctant or unable to investigate and learn from your shame, then overcoming narcissism becomes much harder.

Obstacle five: Fear

Life under a narcissist regime limits your independence. While shame, mind control and weakened self-esteem play an enormous part, it is usually the fear of freedom which stops a person stepping out for good. Having their willpower compromised and being emotionally bullied into a submissive role leaves a target feeling incapable of marching on with an independent life. Even though the current situation is degrading and abusive, they fear the unknown, feeling simply unequipped to handle what a more independent, self-sustaining, dynamic lifestyle might demand of them. They may not believe in their ability to be their own leader.

The narcissist even bases their mind games on fear. They use fear to keep the target compliant. They pull the target's emotional strings and create the illusion that they hold the key to the target's future security. For example, if you express unhappiness about your relationship, the narcissist might give you a 24-hour deadline to 'make up your mind' before they end the relationship. What started as a concern becomes an ultimatum. You begin to feel powerless and crippled by fear.

Obstacle six: Guilt

Guilt is that incessant, gnawing feeling, hacking away at you 24/7. It's like a kick in the guts every time you do something, or say something, or even think something. It is a byproduct of life under a narcissist regime. When you don't act as they expect, the narcissist will continually remind you of the 'sacrifices' they made for you, many of which you never requested. When you can't make it for dinner, but ask who's coming, and are met with "Well, you're not coming, we know that much", it makes you question your loyalty to the narcissist. Their strict expectations of you create numerous collision points for guilt to breed. You feel as though you're always letting them down. Countless instances of these situations lead to habitual guilt being the default emotion accompanying many of the choices you make.

Obstacle seven: Addiction to shamelessness

The most frustrating part of growing in the shadow of narcissism is that you might not be accustomed to 'normal' people who show healthy shame and flaws. Being an 'inverted narcissist' means being addicted to the shameless.

You derive a sense of self when you are serving the narcissist. The concepts of grandiosity and hierarchy become deeply internalised, where you grow accustomed to living under the shadow of a 'superior' person and deferring life's challenges to them. The idea of relationships as equal individuals connecting and offering each other love becomes lost, and you are led to believe that relationships are instead about getting the upper hand and controlling others to obtain scraps of attention for your ego. Spending time with 'regular' humans can then be a jarring experience. 'Regular' people express their fears and concerns, they admit their faults, and they fumble when they speak. And of course they do, they are showing signs of having a range of normal, healthy, human emotion. The narcissist does not exhibit these features; they don't weigh you down with their 'humanity'. This addiction to shamelessness becomes an obstacle to establishing healthy relationships since you might be avoiding the very people who can offer you the empathy and understanding which you need. To overcome this, you will have to take responsibility for yourself. You will then have to grow accustomed to relationships where shame and support are shared; where you can be vulnerable with another person and also be supportive in the face of their vulnerability.

Stay on course

These seven obstacles will come up time and time again. Your job is to be aware of them and to stay on course. When you feel or notice them come up, you will remind yourself that they are just obstacles; conditioned patterns which will fade away the less you react to them. They will feel unpleasant, and because they are emotionally charged, you'll feel that they are gospel. This could not be further from the truth. Feel them, notice them and keep moving forward.

Shattering the myth

The great enemy of the truth is very often not the lie, deliberate, contrived and dishonest, but the myth, persistent, persuasive and unrealistic.

- John F. Kennedy

The battle begins when you accept that the abusive imbalance you have been experiencing between yourself and the narcissist is not what relationships are about. The narcissist has compromised your self-esteem, and they did it by breaking the rules. You didn't have common respect, a shared shame, warmth, understanding and empathy. You tried to play a game of basketball with someone who, instead of bouncing the ball correctly, watching their fouls and respecting the rules, kicked you in the shins then sprinted off and scored the basket. You need to accept that despite this unacceptable style of play, you didn't know better, and continued to respect the rules and play while being walked all over. Now, you will need to break out of the illusion and see narcissism for what it is: a fabrication and a myth. It is a *lie*.

The truth is:

- *The narcissist is **not** better than you*
- *You are **not** incompetent*
- *You do **not** need a person of alleged higher power to navigate through life*
- *Relationships are **not** about playing a role*

The narcissist created these lies and caused you to believe them because you were vulnerable. When you were a child, you were vulnerable. When you are in a relationship and your self-esteem is compromised, you are vulnerable. When you are love starved, you are vulnerable. Relationships, by their very definition, mean being vulnerable. Narcissists take advantage of this.

The battle begins when you shatter this myth and blow it out of the water. You are not worthless and weak. You were coerced into playing with someone who did not respect the rules of the game. Simple as that.

Let the brain re-washing begin

Life, by its very nature, is experiential, meaning our experiences shape our beliefs and behaviours. The problem of narcissism lies at the core of our being. It doesn't change just because we decided or because we read a book. Reversing the damage done by narcissism means creating opposing experiences, and doing them over and over again until they become integrated.

The strategy for making change involves setting a list of goals and working towards them through a variety of practices. This will be a continual process, with progress being made and integrated, followed by more progress and integration. The goals are lighthouses. Instead of meeting those goals, you only need to stay on course and go deeper. The longer you work at it, the more you know, the more experienced you become, the deeper you go and the more natural it will feel.

The road to killing a narcissist consists of seven goals:

1. Healing your toxic shame: Shame as an identity attaches itself to most of your thoughts and urges. You feel shame for wanting something, or for saying something or simply every time you become aware of yourself. The goal will be to face and heal the shame, a little bit at a time, until you begin to free yourself from it. Ultimately, you want to feel shame only when appropriate, and to become accustomed to experiencing it without equating it with inferiority.

2. Coming back to reality: If dissociating is your default mode, you won't be able to take control of your life. The aim is to stay in touch with your true self and your feelings, and to ride through the bumps of life without escaping into the fantasy in your head. Becoming acutely aware of your feelings and your life situation, while initially jarring and painful, will empower you to take control.

3. Mastering your emotions: Shame is one of the most formidable emotions to tame and integrate. As a matter of fact, any emotion can get the better of us. It's important to become aware of a wide array of your emotions and to stick with them, being able to function as you feel them, and to integrate them into a healthy ego. You want to strengthen the mind/emotion connection, where you can feel intense emotions while remaining engaged to your life situation and then make decisions from there.

4. Developing a healthy, well-trained ego: A natural outcome of mastering your emotions is having a wiser, more informed ego. When your emotions are no longer overwhelming you, you will have room to think clearly and effectively. When somebody is attempting to emotionally manipulate you, you will be acutely aware of it. The ultimate reward for mastering your feelings is that you begin to realise that regardless of how you're feeling, you can choose to act in an entirely different direction. This can be difficult to enforce when your feelings keep pulling you in whatever direction they want. Once you have weathered the storm, your healthy ego can function independently of your inner state. You will finally have a choice.

5. Developing a solid, independent sense of self: This is about looking in and finding much more than just overwhelming shame and anxiety. Inside you is a quiet, firm presence which cannot be compromised or affected. Emotions and situations are peripheral compared to this solid, confident self inside you. From this safe space, you will feel like you have backup; a safe, numinous presence to fall back on when things get difficult. Because a solid, independent self cannot be compromised, you will have the power of choice. You won't be dragged in every direction, you will ground yourself in this strong self and view your world from a vantage point.

6. Establishing firm boundaries: The natural outcome of having a solid, independent sense of self is that you will start building boundaries. This will occur naturally. When you begin to feel your true self, you will also begin to protect it. The stronger it gets, the stronger your boundaries. When people (and especially narcissists) test you, they will be met with your strength. They will know that in order to have the best of you, they will need to be fair and respectful.

7. Enjoying your humanity and finding your passion: The true self, once a person connects with it, takes on a life of its own. Instead of incessant anxiety, you'll feel peace. The less you dissociate, the more you'll start to feel your empathy growing and your desire to help others. Weak boundaries keep a person on edge. From your vantage point, you'll feel safety and strength. As a result, you will have the courage to try things you always wanted to do. You'll invest less time and energy on trying to please people and connect deeply with your own needs and desires. A lot of this cannot be explained in words. When the mist begins to clear, you'll experience things that you'd never even imagined. An empowered true self is unique to each person, and how you go about your life from there is unpredictable and exciting. The paradox here is that it will feel completely natural to you. Fear, guilt, anxiety and shame blanket this true self. Once they begin to dissipate, the magic begins.

These seven goals will be gradually realised by utilising the following seven practices, designed to help you move back toward the middle of the shame/grandiosity continuum, both personally and in relationships:

1. **Get allies**
2. **Unleash your true self**
3. **Skill up**
4. **Flex your muscles**
5. **Even the scale**
6. **Boundaries**
7. **Scorched Earth**

Each of these seven practices will incorporate some or all of the seven goals and give you a framework for lasting change. Practice One and Two are the core out of which all practices flow. Without them, the other practices are compromised. The mind-emotion connection is crucial. Withstanding, understanding and accepting your emotions will empower you with the remainder of the practices. You certainly may learn about and begin to implement any of the practices, it's just important that you focus on Practice One and Two initially.

As you utilise the practices, new experiences are created, and your psyche will begin to adapt. Some practices will come easier to you than others. You might already have established some healthy friendships, or boundaries might come easy to you. You might be confident learning and carrying out skill based activities but not feel very confident handling your emotions (or vice versa). The most important thing is that all of the practices are integrated. The practices are about shifting your paradigms i.e. wearing new glasses. Keeping the concepts in your mind will cause you to interpret your experiences in a different way, and with that your beliefs and behaviours will adapt accordingly. Mastering these practices means you might feel like you're getting nowhere for a while, but then suddenly things begin to click. Old beliefs will take over occasionally and muddy the water so that you can't see the way through. That is what it is to attempt a new path. When you start out, you can't see everything. But as you progress, the bigger picture slowly builds. You will take some steps backward and some steps forward. You might have light-bulb moments instantly as you read this book or you might have them later down the track with a little bit of trial and error. But equiped with new knowledge and being aware of the pitfalls and obstacles you might face, you'll have every chance of reclaiming your life from the clutches of the narcissist regime.

Ready? Let's get started.

Practice One: Get allies

A friend is someone who gives you total freedom to be yourself.

- Jim Morrison

Having your emotional world hijacked means that you are no longer in the driver's seat. It's crucial that you have the internal space to think, feel and make decisions independent of another person. It's also important to express your own grandeur and have that seen, as well as release your toxic shame and establish a stronger sense of self. You cannot do this alone. In time, toxic shame takes on its own momentum and begins to function autonomously. A lot of the damage done by the narcissist regime functions autonomously. You cannot climb tall walls without a helping hand from the other side. It's a paradox, but in order to gain autonomy and freedom, you will need support. You will need the help of a set of people who are not narcissists.

Limbic resonance

Limbic resonance is the deepest form of connection two human beings can have. It happens when two people are emotionally engaged and invested in each other. Consider that one person is expressing their sadness about a situation. The other person might start relating to feelings of sadness too, and then, to avoid feeling this way, playfully tells the other person: "Ah, cheer up! It'll be fine!". This is a missed opportunity for limbic resonance. For limbic resonance to occur, the person will need to engage their own feelings as they listen to the other person, and simply stay with the emotion. It's almost trance like. There is a real sense of camaraderie behind it. Quite often, words don't need to be said. The eyes, the facial expression and body posture will communicate that the listener can relate to what the sharer is feeling. The result? The person expressing their emotion will feel deeply and truly understood, and shame is released.

When another person offers you limbic resonance, you will feel accepted and loved at the deepest possible level. Self-esteem increases and the true self begins to come to life. It truly is food for the soul. It's warm and life affirming; it's a lush soil for the true self to thrive in. Connection with a narcissist is cold and life denying; it's hard concrete where nothing can grow. Limbic resonance is a missing ingredient in a relationship with a narcissist. The narcissist is so deeply focussed on their false self that they have no capacity for it. They are far too distracted. Actually, anybody who is afraid of their own emotions won't be able to offer limbic resonance to another person. Many people replace it by playing roles. In such cases, true emotional connection is replaced by mental gymnastics. The dynamic of many families are based on such role playing which is devoid of real substance. Being open to each other's emotional worlds requires a safe space, healthy boundaries, maturity and courage in the face of tumultuous feelings. It requires great patience and skill to establish and maintain such a way of relating to each other.

Many people are not even conscious of what they are missing. A huge chunk of the human population has experienced very minimal amounts of limbic resonance, and as a result, have lost touch with their own humanity. One cannot be truly human without being in touch with their emotions. Without emotions, life becomes a mental abstraction. Having not really felt it, many people are not even aware of the existence of limbic resonance or how desperately they really need it. It is exactly the absence of this phenomena which leaves a person in a love starved state. Without limbic resonance, a person will feel fragmented, depressed, anxious, powerless and hopeless. They are left drowning inside a sticky swamp where life is a cold, dark, uphill climb. Once a person begins to consistently experience limbic resonance, however, balance is restored. They feel whole again, happier, calmer and more upbeat. The true self begins to emerge and life begins to flow in that person. Anxiety fades, and a sense of security and confidence begins to build. It should not be underestimated. Limbic resonance is *crucial*. It doesn't matter how many people you know. Without it, you will find it very difficult to march forward toward your true self.

The hard truth about family

One of the most difficult aspects of change is not having somewhere to turn to for help. The true self needs to feel safe and supported. It needs limbic resonance. When we think of the word 'ally' or 'safe', we think of family. A common misconception is that family is *always* there, and it always gives us exactly what we need. The fact is that while many people do have great support from family, countless more do not have the understanding and guidance they feel they truly need. Some of us live far away from family. Some of us come from emotionally unavailable families that have the best of intentions and which do offer practical support but, due to a lack of limbic resonance during their own upbringing, are unable to offer it to us. And quite simply, some people come from a family littered with narcissists. It can be quite shaming to realise you do not have warm, attuned family to turn to. What's worse, the very people who we grew up worshiping and expecting would love and support us could be the very people who objectified and used us for their own narcissistic supply. Our 'home' might have been compromised, our supply of love poisoned. In these cases, we need allies. We need people who can model family and be as readily available to assist us as possible.

Finding a true ally

Life with a narcissist causes an enormous amount of confusion. You stop knowing what's real. Without a voice of reason, you can go mad pretty quickly. Furthermore, without limbic resonance, narcissism leaves a person in a love starved state. When beginning your work, a therapist can be extremely helpful. Seeing a therapist works on two fronts: Having somebody listen to you empathically instead of belittling your feelings helps you to feel loved and whole, whereas having a person mirror your emotions can help you get a more well rounded grasp on reality. The therapist might raise an eyebrow to odd behaviour which you deem to be normal. This can allow you to question your reality in a safe environment.

The best part of having a therapist is that you can have consistent, reliable access to support. If you have yet to really experience limbic resonance on a consistent basis, you will find it difficult to see what life on the other side of narcissism is like. It becomes harder to escape the clutches of a narcissist. Mind games, guilt and fear create waves of doubt. During your weakest moments, that session with the therapist can refuel you and give you crucial insights as you navigate from psychological bondage to a life of freedom and independence.

The same way toxic shame was brought on through our relationships, shame can only be released in the empathic face of another person. When you interact with your therapist, it is important that you be uncensored. To unravel your shame riddled true self and establish a solid sense of self, you need to feel free to express yourself exactly as you are. What is equally important is that your therapist is open to investing in and experiencing your emotional world. They need to get on the ride and stay with you throughout, regardless of what you are sharing. A narcissist forces you to reject your true self by rejecting it first. Your ally will need to accept *you* and give *you* space to be, and so free you from your psychological cage. While engaging your therapist, it is crucial that you:

- **Speak your thoughts:** No matter how odd your thoughts, or how embarrassing they are, revealing them in a safe environment allows you to release shame and investigate your beliefs at a distance. What you take for granted might not be so 'normal' after all. Also, what might surprise you is that even the most shameful of thoughts lose their power when brought out into the world. The act of sharing can be the most healing part of the journey.
- **Express your emotions:** If you feel an impulse, express it and give it space to exist. If your therapist has done their own internal work, they will be able to empathise and follow along.
- **Stay with your emotions:** Remaining focused on your emotions and not pushing them away is difficult at first, but is a skill which can be learnt. If you can avoid intellectualising an emotion, you open up a space for the possibility of seeing it, feeling it, understanding it and accepting it.
- **Stay conscious:** Going into logic mode (i.e. getting caught up in thought patterns) can disconnect you from

your emotions and stunt growth. Getting caught up in your emotions, on the other hand, can cripple your ability to understand and be rational on a mind level. Therapy can be a safe place for you to connect the two. By allowing and staying with your emotions, you can eventually learn to understand them and express them. Being in touch with difficult feelings while keeping your wits about you is a skill which can be developed, and your session with the therapist is a great place to slow down and practice.

- **Share your hopes and dreams:** Instead of fantasising about your hopes and dreams, begin to vocalise them. The job of the therapist is not to egg you on, but rather to allow you the space to speak up about what's really important to you. They could even provide you with practical suggestions on how to go about achieving them.

- **Face reality:** Coming out of fantasy can be difficult without a mirror. Dissociation and fantasy mean that a person is both lying to themselves and completely unaware of it. A good therapist will gently challenge delusions and help you see your life situation more clearly.

- **Be accountable:** As you share with the therapist, it's important that you stay conscious of your feelings and also that you accept responsibility for your life. Be open to suggestions about better self-care and slow down so the therapist can keep up with you. Many people hold the false preconception that the therapist's job is to 'fix' people. Others use their therapy session as a place to dump their overwhelming emotions without any attempt to understand them and work with them. The job of the therapist is to create a container so that your emotions don't overwhelm you, and to make useful suggestions which help guide you forward. The rest is up to you.

A big part of your success in this practice will depend on your willingness to withstand and learn about your emotions. It also depends on your therapist. If the therapist is tolerant of and capable of withstanding your emotions, and allows them to exist without interfering with the process but while still offering structure and guidance, you will have the psychological space to develop a healthier, more robust sense of self. You will light the fire which feeds the true self.

As you progress, watch out for the mind trap. It can be easy to get caught up re-hashing mental concepts in your head. Instead, continuously look deeper and ask yourself what you are feeling at any one time. Whatever events are happening in your life, while obviously important, are not as crucial as your current emotional state. Only by expressing your true state will you make progress. Staying on the surface or being caught up in the drama of your life will instead keep you stagnant.

Friends

We need friends. More specifically, we need friends who are in it for friendship, not for narcissistic supply. Friends might not be as attuned as a therapist, or as readily available, but they can definitely offer a unique kind of love and acceptance. Unhealthy, unbalanced friendships are harmful to our development. As well as existing to provide us with connection and emotional sustenance, our relationships are about sharing, balance and equality. Also, friendships don't just happen overnight simply because two people both like football. Like learning to drive, you must clock up a certain number of hours and have navigated through a certain number of challenges before the fibres of friendship have been sufficiently bound together. Narcissists will try to sidestep the vulnerability, patience and sacrifice required to build a healthy and lasting relationship.

People to avoid as friends are those who:

- Are too quick to be agreeable and wish to become 'best friends' without clocking up the necessary miles
- Rarely enquire about your life and well-being
- Consistently switch the topic back to themselves

- Play a role that stops any genuine feeling entering the friendship
- Ridicule you and put you down
- Will not emotionally invest in you (offer limbic resonance)
- Sporadically go AWOL but then reappear at a random time

Instead, look for people who:

- Don't use charm to develop a stronger bond with you
- Appreciate a wide array of your qualities
- Laugh with you, not at you
- Accept that physical and emotional space should exist in a friendship
- Can follow along when you express difficult emotions
- Don't place heavy expectations on the friendship
- Make connection the priority and not their own ego
- Behave consistently and openly

Practice Two: Unleash your true self

Be bold, be brave enough to be your true self.

- Queen Latifah

Being in the presence of someone with an inflated ego can limit free expression and corner you into playing a role that is not aligned with your true self. Not only that, but being in the shadow of a narcissist's shamelessness can leave you feeling inferior and incapable. Having a safe, accepting and flexible structure is the only way in which to fully grow your true self.

The great news is that the true self never leaves you, and is always patiently waiting for you to tap into it. It wants nothing more than for you to connect with it and to continually strengthen your bond. In order to effectively connect with the true self, it's important to have a safe space to think and feel, independent of anybody else; narcissist or not. This is an opportunity to put the roles and limiting beliefs aside and to dive in and see what's really in there behind the mask. It allows you to understand and accept all aspects of your subconscious and to integrate them.

Give shape to your true self

Drawing from the principles of Gestalt therapy, the true self can be developed by taking your current emotional state and giving it shape. Gestalt, which is the German word for 'form', focuses on a person's experience in the present moment and allows the person to step back and view themselves from a distance. It's a process of self responsibility and self-awareness. There are a number of activities which you can do that help you connect with your present experience and then inspect it from a distance.

You can:

- **Write a feeling journal:** As you write, don't just rehash what happened during the day. Focus inside on your emotions, and simultaneously decide what to write about. Notice the emotion and then give it shape. Describe what it might look like if it was an object. Journalling is a great extension of therapy and when done correctly and with courage, can be great practice for strengthening the mind/ emotion connection.

- **Write poetry:** Prose is great, yet poetry can give your emotional expression more punch. Follow your impulses and leave the judgements behind. You are not writing for an audience, but for yourself. Explore any theme which appeals to you, no matter how dark.

- **Play an instrument:** Becoming more skilled in an instrument is a wonderful thing, but the greatest thing about music is its ability to resonate with and give expression to your emotions. The bang of a drum can express anger in ways words cannot. The sound of a flute can give flight to your despair in ways speaking about it will not. The string of a guitar can have tingles shooting out of you in ways talking cannot. You can get a hold of an instrument and find a quiet room. You can also hire out a rehearsal room, which will come with instruments. Finally, you can go a step further and partake in music therapy, which can be a powerful way of connecting with emotions under the supervision of a professional.

- **Paint or draw:** Being a great artist is not a prerequisite here. Drawing your emotions can show you things about yourself which you never imagined. It's a way to dream while being awake, giving visual life to your subconscious emotions. The results may surprise you.

- **Sing:** Singing is a great way to connect the effectiveness of music with your voice. By having more intensity in your voice, you can explore emotional frequencies you don't normally feel when talking. You can also pair this with songwriting.

What all of these actives have in common is that they allow you to give shape to your subconscious. It takes what is hidden deep inside and which is acting outside of your conscious awareness, and brings it out into the world. That is, it gives representation to your true self and allows it to be seen. If done well, these exercises will give life to aspects of yourself which you might not initially understand. This is normal and expected. A drawing might confuse you for weeks before you can connect the dots. But when you do connect the dots, you will be more intimate with your true self than you have ever been. This is how growth occurs.

No matter what activity you take up, the important thing is that it is an activity done in a space which is just for you. It's also crucial that you tie the activity into your emotions. When you draw, draw what you're feeling, even if it's abstract and meaningless. Don't just copy another painting or create a portrait of someone. If you play an instrument, let your emotions guide the sound and don't be afraid to lose yourself in the music. Try to leave the thinking mind behind. Lose the structure and pursue things in an organic way, based on what your impulses are telling you. It's not about learning skills and concepts, but about connecting with your emotions, and with that, your true self. Like therapy, it allows you to build the mind/emotion connection, and have a better understanding of how you tick below the thoughts. It's the most efficient way to get to know *you*. When an emotion comes up, you will have the ability to feel it fully, to understand it and to decide how and if to act. This makes you a formidable opponent to anyone looking to manipulate you.

Giving shape to your true self can be uncomfortable, since the emotions you arouse could be negative. Hopefully Practice One with a therapist helped ignite the fire, and you're slowly becoming accustomed to not only permitting your emotions to come out, but to stick with them through good and bad. A sad poem should be just as legitimate as a happy song. A dark, intense drawing is equally as valid as writing about your fun day out and how good it felt. Even a gnawing, never-ending discomfort deserves your care and attention. It's all a part of you, and it all has a right to exist. All of it.

Letting your emotions get out of hand happens to the best of us. Emotions come and go, but *you* remain. When you have developed a certain level of mastery over your emotions, you will have the wit to decide who and what has the right to them. Best of all, you will feel more human and more yourself than you ever have before. There's no limit to how deep you can go.

Sit, and wait

Creative activities are always rewarding, providing an engaging and active path to the true self, which can leave you with tangible representations of your subconscious and allow you to better understand your true self. There is also a more passive path to the true self which is just as rewarding, although at first glance it might not seem like it. It's sitting meditation.

'Self remembrance' is the process of sitting, for a timed period, purely with the aim of allowing a time and space for the true self to emerge. It is a waiting game, and nothing else. The point of self remembrance is to sit with 'you' as long as possible. That's it. You sit there with no expectation of something happening (Although paradoxically, something does eventually happen).

The instructions are as follows:

- Find a quiet room where you will not be distracted.
- Find a spot on the floor and sit cross-legged with your back and neck upright. There is no need for any fancy yoga pose. It helps to have a meditation pillow to sit on, since elevating your torso allows you to maintain good posture and makes the meditation less painful. If you don't have a meditation pillow, you can also stack up some folded towels or clothes and even place a towel under your knees if the ground is hard. The important thing is to establish as much comfort as possible while maintaining a seated, upright position.
- Set a timer. The ideal period is 20 minutes. At first you may need to begin with a much shorter duration and work your way up.
- Rest your hands on each lap.
- Keep your eyes open throughout the sitting. Find a basic object to focus on, such as a cup without printing on it. This will be used as a point of reference throughout the meditation to allow you to gently focus without scattering. If you feel a need to close your eyes, do so, and open them again when you're ready.
- Try to stay relaxed yet focused throughout.

During the meditation, you will hit some difficulties. Sitting perfectly still and silent is a mode the mind does not like very much, and it will rebel. You need to be ready for this.

Exposing the mind, allowing it no distractions and giving it nowhere to go threatens its hold over you. Here is a list of the most common obstacles and how to deal with them:

- **Incessant thoughts:** As you sit, the mind will keep ticking away. This is perfectly fine. You may drift away into your mind and start thinking about the washing, or you could replay parts of the day like a movie, or you could even start analysing the object which you are focussing on. The key is to catch yourself and to gently bring your focus back into the present moment. A good way to ground yourself is to focus on your breath. Breathe 10 slow and deep breaths then go back to a rested, natural state with normal breathing. Another way to centre yourself is to focus in on your body. Focus on your chest area or on your body as a whole, and take notice of how you are feeling. If you catch onto a feeling, go deeper into it and explore it. Give it your attention. Then come back to a relaxed focus when you're ready.
- **Scattering:** When a thought or a stimulation from the outside world causes a strong reaction from the true self, the pain can scare the ego into scattering. During the meditation, the more your true self comes to the surface, the more fear you might experience. As the fear increases, your focus may begin to scatter. The more the true self reveals itself, the stronger your focus must be. You might

also dissociate during the meditation by zoning out or you might get caught up in a thought pattern. The idea is to gently bring your focus back, while being simultaneously aware of your body sensations. It's a balancing act, where too much focus brings too much ego, which blocks the path for the true self. Too little focus causes you to become unconscious, which means the true self will over run you and you won't be able to channel it.

- **Pain and discomfort, including hot flushes:** This will subside with more and more sittings. Over time, your body has stored up all of your buried emotions. When you do the sitting meditation, those emotions will rise to the surface and manifest as pain. You may especially experience it in your shoulders and back. Some gentle stretching after the sitting can help, but just know that in time it will reduce. You may of course stop the meditation if the discomfort becomes too much, but the more you can tolerate the more effective the sitting will be.

- **Doubts and impatience:** The mind will play its games. It will tell you that you're being silly, and that you could better spend your time planning your next holiday. It will think of countless other things you could be doing. It will tell you there is no point to what you're doing. Don't listen to it. It is all a ruse. The mind hates feeling exposed without something to distract it. When these doubts arise (and they will), simply acknowledge them and keep going.

126

- **Foggy vision:** Meditation physically changes your brain chemistry. Foggy vision is a side effect of this, and will settle as you go deeper.

Self remembrance does have an aim: to open a space for your true self to emerge and for you to meet it. However, you will approach the exercise without an aim. The minute you begin attaching an aim to it, you will be energising the mind and so keeping the path to your true self closed. The exercise is about transcending the mind and discovering another realm inside you. You want to be as open and relaxed as possible. Rest assured knowing that the process will unfold by itself; there is nothing you actually need to 'do' but stay focused. You simply sit, and wait. You need to be alert, but rested. It is a paradoxical state, but it will make more and more sense with each sitting.

The fine line between thought and true self

Discovering and exploring the true self is a personal journey and requires faith. Most people spend the majority of their time completely identified with their mind, which consumes their entire reality and stops them from being grounded in something deeper. This lack of grounding makes it easier to be manipulated. The mind can be convinced of anything, the true self, on the other hand, is much harder to fool.

A person may mentally 'know' of the existence of a true self, but knowing does not equate to experiencing. You may 'know of' the city of London, but without actually being there and experiencing its diversity, fast pace and classic landmarks, you will never really actually know it. So it is with the true self. Like a fish in water, when you begin the sitting meditation you will still be in the thinking realm. This is normal. It's the starting point. Without actually having experienced how it is to be truly connected to your true self, you may find yourself thinking that it doesn't actually exist. You must have faith, courage and patience as you find your way toward that wondrous place. There is a *thinking* mode, and there is a *being* mode, and the more sittings you do, the more obvious the line between the two will become. The more faith and courage you show, the more you will be rewarded. A point will come when you do sufficiently uncover it, and you may smile to yourself in acknowledgement. It will be a crucial milestone in your journey, and an enormous piece of the puzzle as you transition out of the narcissist regime and discover your true power.

Practice Three: Skill up

The rules are simple. Take your work, but never yourself, seriously. Pour in the love and whatever skill you have, it will come out.

- Chuck Jones

Reclaiming your true self is extremely empowering. When you begin to engage your emotions and allow them space to breathe, you'll begin to notice that they also allow you to harness more energy. It works in two ways; you won't be wasting your energy trying to suppress your emotions, and by being allowed to come to the surface, your emotions will energise you.

Also, living within the confines of a narcissist regime would have held you back from being your own leader. Leaders carve out new paths. Leaders walk bravely into the unknown. Leaders have skills. You are that leader, even though you might not have fully realised your potential. You have big shoes fill. This practice is about filling said shoes.

Living up to your potential means growth. Growth involves confronting truths and dealing with a range of uncomfortable emotions. Through Practice One and Two, you will have laid a foundation for handling your emotions with more maturity than ever before. From there, you can begin to build more life competence, and in doing so, you'll begin to put the myth of narcissism to the test. You are indeed capable. This is not about one-upping other people, this is about raising your own personal bar. Becoming more life competent means gaining useful skills and doing activities that build internal strength and resilience. By slowly increasing your life skills, you will be disproving your limiting beliefs. What you do and how you do it depends on you, your life situation and your taste.

Some suggestions are:

- **Travel alone:** This can be the most daunting and the most rewarding of things to do. Very few activities call on you to learn more new skills on the fly (pun intended) than travel. Knowing what to pack, organising your time, deciding what to do and for how long to do it, being forced to communicate in alternative ways, learning about new cultures and ways of living; the list is endless. When you travel to foreign lands and find yourself in unfamiliar situations, your mind will need to adapt in ways it never had to before and your true self will be aroused like never before. You will remember what it is to see the world with 'new eyes'.

- **Learn a language:** Learning a new language means expressing yourself in a completely new way. Your brain will change, and as you become more fluent, your way of seeing yourself will change. Your identity will evolve, and your confidence will grow. It obviously helps to be in the country where the language is spoken, but even if you are learning from home, it's definitely still possible. There are language apps you can download. You can listen to music, watch movies and read newspapers and books. Choose a culture you are genuinely curious about and work away at it. In time, you'll find yourself inching closer to fluency.

- **Martial arts:** A great way to connect mind and body. For those unaccustomed to honing their strength, Martial Arts can empower you and build confidence.

- **Take cooking classes:** For the uninitiated, learning to cook is both a skill and a form of self love. Even knowing a few dishes can go far.

- **Take a wine or whiskey tasting class:** Appreciating alcohol by learning the history and theory, as well as being able to connect this knowledge with various types of wine/whiskey can add sophistication to your social life. Everyone knows how to get drunk, not everyone knows their drink.

- **Read psychology or philosophy books:** Reading books on shame and vulnerability, philosophy books such as Schopenhauer's 'World as Will and Representation' or Paulo Coelho's 'The Alchemist' can expand your perspective and give you a greater appreciation of world and mind.
- **Update your tech skills:** For those not in the field, technology can seem like a no-go zone; only for the brainiacs. Taking a basic website or programming course, or even something as simple as touch typing, can shine a light on the craft of the geek. You would be surprised how creative it is and how much imagination it requires.
- **Take a photography course or workshop:** Learn how to see and how to capture the world around you. Almost everybody takes snaps with their smartphone these days, not everyone learns the art behind it.
- **Learn an instrument:** There are countless video tutorials and resources online for you to learn the basics. You could also learn the music to your favourite songs to make it more interesting.
- **Play a sport:** You can study and practice the skills which a sport requires. This gives you a way to combine fun with discipline and to build more confidence.

Standing out in the open, in total darkness, with nobody ahead of you to tell you where you should go and being expected to find a way through is one of the most daunting feelings one can have. Becoming the person who welcomes such situations into their life, however, is well within the realm of your ability.

As you become more and more competent in an array of life skills, your capacity and confidence will grow. You'll slowly begin to realise that somewhere inside you there is a source of energy and wisdom which you never imagined existed. Confidence breeds confidence, and you'll find that you trust yourself to handle new challenges. As mentioned earlier, Practices One and Two will complement this practice, because learning a skill takes patience and physical as well as emotional grit. You will have days where the skills don't come easily, and you will need to persist through feelings of shame, frustration and unworthiness. Pressing on and learning to act despite the emotional storm inside is how you will succeed in this practice.

Mastery is a conscious *and* an unconscious act. Each hour you consciously invest in service of your chosen field will add up on an invisible calculator. Before you've even realised it, you'll find yourself becoming very competent. It's always a pleasant surprise. Those moments where you realise how far you've come will encourage you to go even further, and as the fog of doubt and shame slowly dissipates, you will become more and more aware of your own potential for growth. There is no better way to develop shame tolerance than through skill building. Building competence means facing your limits up close, over and over again. Through this process, you become more accepting of your human limits and paradoxically, more aware of your inner potential. There is no end to this process, it only goes deeper and deeper.

Practice Four: Flex your muscles

Be sure you put your feet in the right place, then stand firm.

- Abraham Lincoln

Like a strain of flu, we can protect ourselves from victimisation by a narcissist if we vaccinate ourselves. Yes, to become more narcissist proof, we inject ourselves with narcissism.

Firstly, don't worry; there are no needles involved. Secondly, don't be afraid you'll develop full-blown narcissistic personality disorder. You are biologically different. You have been blessed with the ability to feel shame and guilt. If these emotions were inserted like a chip in our brains, then narcissists would have an empty slot. So no matter what you do, you will never be a full blown narcissist. As long as you are in touch with those emotions, you will remain grounded. Recall that narcissism exists on a continuum, and even though we may slide up and down the scale, we can always bring ourselves back to the middle.

The incessant shaming by a narcissist convinces the target that they are unworthy and incapable. This leads to a lack of belief in their grandeur, except of course when they dissociate and fantasise. Taking up more space and standing out as the special one in the real world is a foreign concept which they usually designate for others. The remedy? Start being a little more narcissistic yourself. Stop imagining that you are special and start exercising your specialness. It will make you feel exposed and afraid, since you could in some situations be met with resistance, but it's something you can grow accustomed to. After all, what could be more natural than living out precisely what life wants you to? Practice One through to Three serve to give you a more realistic view of yourself and should raise your self-esteem to where it's supposed to be. Your behaviour should simply be an extension of that.

Be special, be fair

Full blown narcissism is grandiosity gone wrong. It is grandiosity addiction and it works by shaming others. Channelling your grandeur, when done with respect, can help you contribute to your world. As well as being a human being with flaws and limits, you are also inherently special and capable of amazing things, and you're definitely allowed to channel that.

There's nothing nicer than seeing a person with humility and humanity who inherently believes they are special. There is nothing wrong with loving yourself and having abundant self-esteem. There is a lot wrong with believing you are God and then objectifying everyone as a result. Keeping in mind the difference between grandeur and grandiosity, you can:

- **Go public:** Give your opinion more, offer to give a presentation at work, share your creative work with the world or host events such as a birthday party or a house warming. As you come across friction from the world or from people, be open and listen, make adjustments if necessary, then keep doing it. Think of it as you contributing to your world. When done with humility and in a way which gives value to others, people will appreciate it.
- **Take control:** Don't always leave it up to others to plan and be in charge. Make suggestions about where to go for dinner or create the plans and lead the way. There is a fine line between being bossy and contributing to your relationships. Find it. Try to understand who you're planning for and find things which intersect for all

involved. Strength and understanding are a great combination in relationships. When you can assert yourself in a way which enhances the lives of others, people will feel secure in your presence. Be that presence.

- **Dream big:** Come up with ideas about things you're passionate about and think up ways to bring them to life. Don't be abashed; you're dreaming big because you are inherently big. Think of the smallest possible step you can take and take it. Do it daily, and as you put in more time, the representation of that dream will become clearer in the real world. Acknowledge your setbacks and obstacles and then find ways around them. Dreaming big and then doing something each day in service of that is how you make an impact on the world. It doesn't really matter what it is, when you're in touch with your true self, you'll be skilled at following your instinct and you won't need any reassurance about why you're doing it.

- **Have a sense of entitlement:** Take the last slice of cake (someone has to), say sorry less, don't hug the wall so much when you pass someone in the hallway and talk a bit louder. Make strong eye contact. This world is yours too.

If skilling up (Practice Three) brought you face to face with your shame, this practice will toss you into the deep end. It's one thing to face your limits in daily practice, it is another thing entirely to stand out and open yourself up to the critique of others. Creating art and making it public is inviting the world to see your heart and soul. Speaking up and standing out from others can ruffle feathers, especially those of narcissists. Lifetime wounds can be reopened. Exposing your true self and feeling judged and rejected is painful. Shame can run riot in these situations. The trick is to go slow, and to be courageous. It also helps to make full use of Practice One (Allies) during those moments when you're feeling vulnerable and exposed. Standing out and making yourself vulnerable in the real world is easier when you can get the support and understanding of those people who are in your corner. Your allies can tell you when you've gone too far, or they can help you see that the very thing you feel most ashamed about isn't such a big deal. They can also cheer you on in their own way and encourage you when the chips are down. Your allies can give you the perspective and support to persevere through this practice until it becomes natural. Also, as your sense of self grows, you'll have a firm cushion to press against for comfort when you run into difficult times. Setbacks and challenges won't destroy your willpower so easily. You'll need no excuses, because you have already made your pact with life. In the face of all obstacles, you'll know that you are simply doing what you were put on this Earth to do.

Go forth and conquer... your shame

It's hard to develop healthy narcissism if you feel that you're not even special. But once that belief slowly dissipates, you'll start to realise that you are indeed infinitely special. You'll begin to realise that a lot of the shame you previously felt wasn't even necessary; it was only keeping you contained in a psychological cage. You'll also learn that we live in a world of abundance, where being special doesn't equate to putting others down or being a narcissistic asshole. It just means staking your claim. When you assert yourself like this, rather than seeing a sheep they can control, the narcissist will see someone they can fear. And the world will see someone they can admire.

Practice Five: Even the scale

I feel beautiful when I'm at peace with myself. When I'm serene, when I'm a good person, when I've been considerate of others.

- Elle Macpherson

A relationship with a narcissist is lopsided. Their plans always have priority. In a conversation, their voice has priority. When you try to influence them, they put up massive walls. Unless it serves their interest, they say no.

Your lifelong mission is to cultivate relationships where the scale is even. It's a skill which takes time to hone. If you've been in contact with narcissists most of your life, you might have lost sight of what balance looks like in a relationship. You might be the kind of person who always says yes, and then brushes it off when the other person keeps saying no to you. You might sit quietly, and listen empathically for hours, help the other person with their issues, but when you assert your opinions or problems, you're met with a blank stare and a dismissive comment.

The emotional investment mismatch

When you're not conscious of it, the narcissist's refusal to be vulnerable creates an *emotional investment mismatch*. Narcissists don't believe in mirroring emotions. That would involve the true self. Their only way of relating is to have you mirror their false self. When two people normally connect, the person listening would raise their emotional intensity to that of their partner, hence achieving limbic resonance. When you are in 'connection' with a narcissist, you don't get any emotional feedback, so you try harder to get your message across. Instead of investing their true self, the narcissist will dismiss the emotional content of your message. They will instead analyse your words and then speak about them from their point of view. Before you know it, the tide has turned, and you are left mirroring the narcissist.

The emotional investment mismatch can have damaging effects on the target. The target grows to think that emotional resonance is a scarce commodity and that if you want people to hear you, you need to force your way into the listener's mind. If you live with narcissism for long enough, you develop a habit of expecting an emotional investment mismatch. When you are in an open exchange with others, you might end up raising the intensity of your emotions and not give them a chance to match and connect. You might speak at people like you would a narcissist and try to force the emotional content on them, hoping it gets through quickly before they can cut you off. The problem with having your emotional laser on full power, however, is that the other person does not have the space to connect and resonate with you.

Balanced connection can only occur when:

- The speaker spoon feeds the listener their intention, giving them time to mentally grasp the message and connect emotionally with the intention of the message.
- The listener can hold their thoughts and allow the speaker's intention to impact their true self, giving ample space for the speaker to express themselves.
- The speaker allows space for the listener to chime in and ask questions to better help the listener grasp their intention.
- Both people are equally aware of the emotional resonance behind the conversation and can balance the intensity.

Keep in mind that emotional investment is not the same as speaking. A narcissist can talk for a long period of time without actually investing real vulnerability into the exchange. What they are effectively doing is using their false self as a smoke screen. Emotional investment is felt. For example, you could begin telling a story about your pet who recently died. The story is one thing, the expression of sadness behind the story is another. Also, the other person's response is one thing, and whether they are empathising with your sadness is another. In an exchange, you can either leave feeling understood or be left feeling like you were never actually heard; even after the other person responded. It's the *emotion* behind the exchange which matters.

If the person you are interacting with refuses to accept and match your level of emotional investment, even after you've given them the space to do so, or continually hijacks the conversation, then it's best to end the interaction. Without equal mirroring, shame will arise.

The emotional investment trap

The narcissist wants you invested. They have you stuck in a loop of trying, being disappointed and then trying again. Over time, this wears down your self-esteem and leaves you in a love-starved state. Empathising, listening and understanding are how we show love. Being on the receiving end of this recharges us. Like food or air, the true self needs this to thrive. The narcissist thrives on this too, but in a different way. Investing in them gives them an ego boost and feeds their narcissistic supply. It doesn't matter if you're empathising with them or you're defending yourself over something they said; as long as you're engaged, you are feeding them narcissistic supply. In their case, however, it can never be filled.

If you start losing interest in them, the narcissist will feed you morsels of fake love and charm to keep you on the hook. They will pretend to empathise and understand, to pull you back into believing that you can achieve balance. If that doesn't work, they'll create drama to obtain your engagement. They might randomly declare that you've been distant or preoccupied. They could subtly poke fun at you. Then the minute you react and re-engage emotionally, they resume sucking you dry for their narcissistic supply. That's the trap.

Bringing emotional balance back to a relationship with a narcissist is pretty much impossible. Trying to find it there is like trying to find water in a desert. The way to bring emotional balance back to your life is by *finding people who are capable of balanced emotional investment*. By spending more time with such people, you eventually start to see the difference between narcissists and those with healthy shame and empathy. When it becomes clear to you, it's like night and day. Spend long enough living in darkness, and it's only normal you forget how daylight feels.

The humour trap

A narcissist will use humour as a way to control. They might laugh when saying something mundane, just to get you to laugh along. It's a game of "When I say haha you say ha". You could be mistaken for thinking it was a nervous tick because it happens so often and without any real cause. Being polite and aware of social norms, you laugh too, unconscious of the fact that you might not even think what the narcissist said was funny.

Narcissists also hide ridicule in humour. Because they say it in a playful way, and often in the presence of a group of people, you feel coerced into laughing along. When this is done long enough, you eventually start downplaying yourself and laughing at yourself in the presence of the narcissist. Over time, you can be conditioned to put yourself down and accept being put down by others.

The solution to this problem? Stop laughing. It's not funny. You don't have to laugh every time someone else does. You definitely do not have to laugh when you are the subject of ridicule. If you're in a relationship where back and forth banter is the norm, then go for it. Banter can spice up a friendship. But doing it with a narcissist is pointless since they will turn it into a competition. If you are always the butt of the jokes, or you realise that behind the jokes the content is actually hurtful and making you feel small, then just refuse to laugh. By not laughing along, you take the power away from the narcissist.

The conversation trap

When the target is always investing, then the narcissist won't need to say much. It's usually a waiting game, where if they leave enough space, the target will be inclined to fill it.

Many narcissists, however, use conversation as a form of control. They will usually begin by enquiring about your life, asking how you are doing or how work is going. Once you become engaged, they swiftly turn the focus back on themselves and keep it there. They then hit you with a barrage of words which trap you, stringing together a never-ending series of mental concepts which barely relate to you. A lot of words are spoken, but not much is said. You then feel trapped because you're too polite to interrupt, as your frustration and despair continue to build.

Speaking to the narcissist makes you feel like you don't even exist and leaves you feeling frustrated and used. Conversation should be a sparring session of back and forth sharing. The limelight should be shared and the interest mutual. The emotional investment should be equal on both sides. A good conversation can warm the heart and feed the soul. A conversation with a narcissist can leave your brain feeling as though it has been under siege by a machine gun that fires words. It's empty and mentally exhausting. Such conversations should be cut short at all costs.

Practice Six: Boundaries

We can trust ourselves to know when our boundaries are being violated.

- Melody Beattie

Hanna had terrible stomach cramping. She had been putting in 11 hour days at work for a few weeks, and her boss kept handing her more and more tasks to do. A task which would take a whole day was expected to be done in a couple of hours, as well as a handful of other tasks. Hanna was the only one in the company capable of doing such work, and so she took the tasks on without any resistance. Most days, she skipped her lunch break and ate her food at her desk. She felt anxious because she could never quite catch up with her work. In truth, she was expected to do the work of two people. She hadn't been sleeping well and had been feeling resentful about being pushed around to do her boss's bidding. The human resources manager noticed her discomfort one day and sent her home to rest. After half a day off, she stumbled back to the office the next day and resumed working. The pain in her stomach had reduced a bit but still caused her discomfort. She felt stuck - and very sad.

Stories like Hanna's are common. Nobody can do anything because the person being mistreated doesn't speak up. Quite often they don't feel they have a choice. Any person with an idea about boundaries would know how to handle such a situation. They would ensure they only put in eight hour work days and overtime would be the exception, not the rule. They would take a full lunch break. They would clearly state how long a task takes to do and would reject a task with an unreasonable deadline or push it back until the workload was manageable. They would let management know that the system is not working and that they will not play the martyr. They would speak up.

When a narcissist has you picked out as their target, they expect that you do what they want, when they want it. They have very little regard for your rights and boundaries. They see you as an object they can use. If they want to go to the party and want you to come with them, they will pile on the pressure until you submit, regardless of how you feel. If you express sickness or weakness, they start wishing you would just get over it and keep doing what they want. They get very excited when they realise somebody has weak boundaries.

They expect you to be an open book. They need to know everything you're doing, thinking and feeling. They feel entitled to every inch of you. It can be difficult to know where you end and where they begin. The longer it's been happening, the more difficult it is to become aware of it.

If you have weak boundaries, you will have problems. The people who respect you will allow you a standard set of boundaries even if you don't ask for them. A part of those people will still wish that you could be clearer about what is ok and what isn't. It makes even the most respectful of people nervous.

The narcissist, on the other hand, will see it as an open invitation to have their way with you. They will test the limits with most people they meet until they find a way to influence them. It's like a series of doors in a building. They will check them one by one until they find one which is unlocked. And the less you say no, the more they will push.

Having something to defend

The obvious requirement for boundary setting is that you need to have something to protect. Like a fence around a block of land, you need a solid sense of self before you can create a boundary around it. When you focus inside, you need to experience inner peace and strength. You need to meet with something that tells you exactly who you are. Practice One and Two are designed to help you do this. Note that we do not include Practice Three. It's not what you can do which gives you a sense of self, but rather a deep and abiding connection to your true self which gives you your identity.

When a narcissist insists on something from you, your first reaction would be to search inside yourself for an answer to their demand. If you find only anxiety and fear, or you feel fragmented and cut off from your true self, you will feel like you have no choice. You will succumb. You will feel suffocated and full of despair.

With a sense of self, on the other hand, you will know yourself as an individual with needs and wants. When you feel this solid sense of separateness, you will know that your internal state and what you want at a certain moment can be different to the other person - and that it's ok. If a person wants you to have Vietnamese with them, but you had some the night before and instead crave something a bit heavier, you will know that their demand is not what is right for you at that moment. If the narcissist opens your mail, you will feel that it's none of their business to be doing so and let them know. If your narcissist boss tells you spontaneously they want you to finish a new task at 6:00 pm on a Friday night, and you just want to get home and spend time with family, you will feel that it's time to speak up.

You are an individual. Only you know what's right for you, and your state at a certain time can be different to other people. Being raised in a way where boundaries are not an option is abuse. Being treated like a person who does not get a say is abuse. It is a basic human right which all people must have. Yet there is no personal boundaries police. Abusing another person's emotional boundaries is not a crime. *It's up to you to enforce them.*

Keep in mind that a certain boundary can apply one day and not apply the next. In the example of the Vietnamese, you might be craving Vietnamese that day, and so you could agree to a request to have some. Knowing your true self and your mind, body and spirit informs you of which boundaries you need to set. Normally when there is a discrepancy between what you allowed and how much you were actually willing to accept, you will sense it as a sick feeling in your stomach. It's important to know your state before you make a decision. Once you weigh up how you feel, you then have a multitude of choices:

- Say yes, knowing it's 100% ok with you
- Say no, without excuses, wholeheartedly knowing it's not what you want
- Say yes, but with a set of conditions, knowing that in order to feel comfortable saying yes, you need to adjust the person's request
- Say no, but with a concession, where you state that although you're saying no, you are willing to go along with part of the request or take a rain check
- Say "I don't know". When we are overwhelmed by life or by our emotions, sometimes we simply do not know what we want in that specific moment. It's important to feel ok with that. "I don't know, give me an hour to decide" is also a valid response, especially when you are consciously just starting to set boundaries. A firm 'no' should result if anybody tries to coerce you into giving them an answer immediately.

Any invasion of your mental and emotional space is never ok, and it is your job to protect that space. It's also your job to recognise the guilt that arises when you say no and be able to cope with and process it. Boundaries are about two people gently pushing against each other and trying to find a balance. If one person pushes too hard, it's the job of the other person to push back gently. That sick feeling of entrapment and resentment normally arises if you say yes to something you don't want, so that's rarely a good option. A 'no' creates choices. A reluctant yes is passive and causes self-harm, a no is informative and useful for both parties. Learning to use it can empower both you and your relationships.

You can also negotiate a request. It starts with knowing what your true self wants at any given moment. As you begin to master this skill, you can use what your instincts are telling you and weigh up the situation. Occasionally, for the good of those we love, we might go along with their request regardless. But you might be surprised how often a person would welcome your boundaries and be able to cooperate with you to ensure both parties are satisfied. Even a narcissist will eventually have to accept a boundary. They will loathe it, and they might fight it, but knowing that you mean business, they will accept it.

Blowing your top

Coming out of subjugation, establishing a solid sense of self, and then beginning to set boundaries doesn't always go smoothly. When you come to terms with how long the narcissist abused your right to set boundaries, you might discover your rage rising to the top. You might go through a stage where you want to say no outright to everything anybody asks of you. It can be hard to tell who's taking advantage of you and who's not, and which requests are reasonable - especially when the narcissist is being charming.

This angry phase, if you go through it, will eventually pass. Sometimes, as you're discovering your sense of self, you might need to set unreasonably strict boundaries just to test the extremes. You might need to spend an unreasonable amount of time alone and say no a lot. You might need to cut out all stresses and pressure just to keep up with your emotions. Going into lockdown might be just what you need for that time. Remember, boundary setting is about knowing your state at any given time and deciding from there. If your state of mind and body is telling you that you're angry and want to say no to everyone, then so be it. If it's telling you that you're overwhelmed and can't think straight enough to give an answer at that moment, then that's how it has to be. There is never one right path; it depends on many factors. The right path one day could be the wrong one the next. It's all about knowing and accepting your state in the moment.

As you improve and start setting firm boundaries, you'll notice those who care about you respecting you more, and narcissists leaving you alone more. You'll become more intimate with your true self and start becoming more protective of your own interests.

Enough is enough

One subtle form of boundary setting which is usually not utilised by the target of narcissists is the ability to say enough. Targets feel obligated to give up their time, even when they don't want to. The power the narcissist has over them is usually too strong, and they feel that they have no choice. Being dragged along shopping, feeling obligated to stay longer at social events or being sucked into listening to incessant chatter can be suffocating. Without boundaries, the target's feeling of powerlessness will leave them with a painful sense of despair. Boundary setting is not just about saying no, but also about deciding how much of our time and resources we want to offer others. It's about giving our true self more say, and our sense of obligation and guilt less power over us.

Saying enough should not be black and white. Quite often we can remain in a situation but change the terms of engagement. We can go shopping with somebody but use some of that time to seek out stuff we want. We don't need to say no to going to a social event, but when we feel enough is enough we can make arrangements to leave. We can speak with a person then politely end the conversation when it gets too much. When on holiday, we can state that we need a few hours of downtime to relax before going exploring. If the people in our life love us, they will be flexible and open to negotiating each situation so that everyone is comfortable. It's a dynamic process. We feel what we feel, and we prefer what we prefer. We are all unique. We have the right to change the situation to suit our internal state better. When we do it in service of our true self, we never have to feel guilty.

Furthermore, watch out for any mind games a narcissist plays when it comes to setting boundaries. They may attempt to make you feel foolish about your boundaries, and try to convince you that other people don't set those same boundaries. They might create a list of compelling reasons why you must cooperate and try to corner you into yielding. It's crucial that you leave behind the world of right or wrong and to understand that the word of the narcissist is not gospel, only the word of your true self is.

Practice Seven: Scorched Earth

I take the invasion of my personal space very seriously.

- Kid Rock

Scorched Earth is a military strategy used by a people when the enemy is advancing on their territory. Anything of use to the enemy such as houses, food, vehicles, utilities or equipment is burnt, leaving nothing which could help the enemy sustain their assault.

Having empathy for others endears them to us. In many cases, this is what we want. When it comes to narcissists, we need them endeared to us like we need to be run over by a truck. Yes, narcissists are often wounded people and maintaining a false self is painful for them. But believing they can change or trying to have them play fair never works. We must refuse to play the game. We do this by disengaging from our emotions. Remember, the game is in play as long as our emotions bind us to the other person. The act of disengaging from our emotions effectively ends the game. To emotionally disconnect from a narcissist is to starve them of their power over us. And we do this with *contempt.*

Contempt is a state of disapproval, where we see the other person as not living up to our personal standards. Contempt is the cool kid at school looking down on the supposedly not so cool kid. Contempt is the person who makes us cringe because they are so nice it hurts. Contempt is felt toward the guy at a social gathering who joins a circle of friends that have known each other for years and pretends to be one of the guys.

In your case, you can view yourself as a person of integrity, healthy shame and healthy guilt; a person with a moral compass who plays fair. You can then view the narcissist with contempt, i.e. as a person who;

- lacks integrity, healthy shame, healthy guilt and a moral compass
- doesn't play by the rules
- has little capacity for change, self-reflection or growth

By mentally reframing where you stand in relation to the narcissist, by raising the standards for your relationships, you can place the narcissist in a box where your emotions can't enter.

Being emotionally cut off from people is unpleasant and inhumane. Contempt is never a good thing. It's a wilderness without warmth. It's an enormous wall created by a person to keep them being 'stained' by those who they hold in contempt, that is, the person who they view as beneath their standards; whatever those standards may be. But in the case of our narcissistic relationships, it's like getting chemo for our cancer. Scorched Earth. The game ends abruptly. We can instead choose to invest our emotions into healthier, more nourishing relationships. Only then will the drama end.

It's important to note that disconnecting from your emotions is not easy. But the key here is to do it strategically. As much as we like to believe that we need always to be empathic and open, when somebody is overtly abusing us and taking advantage of our emotions, they quite simply don't deserve to be let in. This is not to say that the narcissist will just surrender and play nice. They want to make good on their investment of time. They will make attempts to pull you back in. They might get angry or give you the silent treatment. They might accuse you of being insensitive. They might play the victim or play sad. They will do their utmost to make you feel guilty. Our compassion will always push us to engage with people who we see suffering and to soften our stance. The narcissist is aware of this and will play on it. It is crucial that you see the impulse come up, acknowledge it and then continue as normal.

If a narcissist is to remain in your life for the foreseeable future, then Scorched Earth is to be used whenever you sense a manipulation coming on. As you begin to see the narcissist more clearly, you'll start to feel a strong need for emotional boundaries.

Don't touch the hot potato

It's not just overt invasions which we must protect against, but also covert ones. As explained earlier, shaming can occur in many ways which are subtle and passive. When a person attempts to shame another, it's like they are handing that person a hot potato. It burns. The key is to either refuse to take the hot potato or to hand it back.

If the narcissist accuses you of doing something or not doing something, they could be doing this just to garner a reaction. It's important to spot it and then save the emotional response. Scorched Earth involves trying to separate the emotion from the fact. If what they accuse you of has no substance, then you can hand back the hot potato by calmly stating that they are entitled to their opinion, but you don't agree with what they say. Even if the narcissist's accusations have some substance, you can take their criticism on board and decide whether it requires action. Quite often, the emotional reaction overwhelms all reason and puts a smoke screen over the actual problem: the narcissist is trying to shame you. Your emotional outburst is exactly what the narcissist is counting on. They want you to engage your emotions and take hold of the hot potato. If you respond calmly and with reason instead, you keep the power in your hands, and you make the narcissist accountable.

The narcissist may try to shame you by teasing you or putting you down. You can avoid the hot potato in various ways:

- Don't reinforce what they say and don't laugh along
- Don't try to justify yourself or to shame them back
- If you feel a need to act, then simply question their motives. Ask them what they mean exactly, and ask them to justify their comments. Treat it like an interview. Respond to them in a business-like fashion. Be matter of fact.

- If you are affected by the narcissist, wait until later and then consult a close ally and ask them to verify if the narcissist's words have any substance.

Avoiding the hot potato is a process of withholding an emotional response and instead switching to the rational realm. Rather than feeling what the narcissist says or seeking limbic resonance in your interaction with them, you can instead analyse it in your mind and test it for any grain of truth. Your emotional response feeds the narcissist, questioning them and refusing to play along diffuses their game and evens the playing field. Avoiding the hot potato is about analysing and processing every word that comes out of the narcissist's mouth. It's about being a buzzkill and making no excuses for the fact.

Refuse to take the bait

Karen handed over the keys to her landlord after he had carried out the final inspection. He had been friendly, swift and cooperative.

In the weeks leading up to the handover, her landlord had demanded that she forfeit $200 of her bond money for 'oven cleaning', which was not stated in the contract. When she refused, he sent her numerous aggressive and personal emails explaining how she needed to cooperate with his demands and how she was being 'childish'. He questioned 'what her mother would think' and made rude references about her lack of cleanliness, calling her a 'dirty little girl'. Karen was shocked. Why did a business relationship turn personal all of a sudden? Nobody of sound mind would behave in such a way. Finally, afraid of what might come next, she relented and decided to agree to the oven cleaning fee, even though it was not in the contract and not justified. Feeling unsafe to be alone with the landlord, Karen decided to ask a male friend to attend the apartment handover.

Everything went well, and with Karen's male friend being present, the landlord was on his best behaviour. Not surprisingly, a day after the handover, Karen received the most scathing email yet, which was in stark contrast to how the landlord had behaved the previous day at the handover. He again made personal remarks about her hygiene, going as far as to say that she was 'disgusting'. He questioned how she could even live in such 'filth' and then proceeded to make further remarks about how Karen's mother would be ashamed of her, even though he did not know Karen's mother. He had said nothing at the handover in the presence of Karen's male friend and had even signed a paper saying that everything was fine. Karen was understandably shocked and confused. What the hell was going on? she thought. How should she respond to this email?

Firstly, it would be impossible for Karen to understand *why* her landlord was behaving like this. What was clear, however, was that this man was a narcissist. His judging, attacking tone and outlandish statements were a testament to that. He thrived while enforcing his power over young women. He had been open with Karen about the fact that he only tolerated young women in his apartment. It seemed he loved to stir chaos in the minds and hearts of his tenants.

Karen had many ideas about how to respond to the email; she wanted to explain that she had cleaned the apartment well, that he was being hurtful and that what he said was unsubstantiated. She wanted to ask why he mentioned nothing during the handover when her friend was present. She had so many things to say and ask. Then she recalled the first incident with the oven cleaning. Engaging the landlord's game had only aroused more of his anger, and he had simply piled on more drama and insults.

Karen knew what to do. She showed the email to some friends who had been to her apartment in the week before she moved out and had been at her place many times and knew how clean she actually was. They all agreed he was a madman and were confused as to why he would send an email with such odd insults. Everything he said was subjective and unsubstantiated. Reassured that she was not crazy, that she was not disgusting, and that she was not living in filth (nor had she ever), she opted for radio silence. Her emotions were one thing, the right action was another. She left it. No response. No questions. No defence. She knew that her landlord was fishing for an emotional response in order to feed his narcissistic supply. Making her squirm and wriggle was his intention. There was no other point to his email.

She refused to take the bait.

While still extremely shaken up and hurt, she decided simply to move on with her week. She would not engage the drama. She would direct any unresolved emotion regarding the situation to a close friend or her therapist or write about it in her journal. She had moved to her new apartment, and her new landlord was by all measures friendly and cooperative. If her narcissist landlord would give her trouble about anything contractual, then she would communicate with him only regarding that, with no emotional charge. She would involve lawyers if need be. If he sent more emails personally insulting her, she would *say nothing*. If he behaved criminally in any way or made any threats, she would call the police. Scorched Earth.

The Blame Game

Living well is the best revenge.

- George Herbert

Being on the receiving end of narcissism generates bucket loads of rage and frustration. For some of us, it began in childhood by the very people entrusted to care for us when we had no say. Some of us let down our guard while assuming the golden rule and spent years embroiled in drama and emotional misery before finally waking up to the truth. But now the cat is out of the bag. You look down on this dark, horrible truth, feeling used and full of anger. You point your finger. You need an object of rage for all the wasted time and needless suffering.

While we can blame the narcissists in our life, we can also foolishly turn on ourselves. We can blame ourselves for falling for the mind games. We can question why we endured the put downs and tolerated our needs being ignored. We can ask why we settled for less and allowed ourselves to be sucked back in when a part of us was screaming at us to walk away. We could also blame ourselves for the fact that, despite now being adults with free will, we still walk into relationships with narcissists.

Yes, your anger is justified. You have been wronged. Yes, if you feel a need to express your anger, you should find ways to do so. Yet blaming the narcissist keeps the focus outside of yourself and keeps you distracted from pursuing freedom. Your outrage *empowers* the narcissist. This uselessness of your outrage can be the most enraging part of all. Furthermore, blaming yourself instead keeps you in a self-destructive state of mind, and also distracts you from the task at hand. When you have been conditioned to play a certain role and previously had known no other way, then the blame is not on you. It is a difficult yet necessary paradigm shift; blame is not what you should be seeking at all. Finger pointing will not fix it. On the contrary, your freedom and empowerment are where your energy will be best spent. You can channel your outrage in a multitude of healthy and creative ways that directly benefit and improve your life.

Trust, but verify

"Trust, but verify" is a Russian proverb which Ronald Reagan used as one of his signature phrases. It holds a lot of truth in many aspects of life, and no less in dealing with narcissism.

Life is not black and white. We can sometimes pigeonhole people who don't necessarily deserve it. We all have elements of narcissism in us, and that can sometimes get the better of us. Narcissism exists on a continuum; it's different for everyone. We all have to deal with this reality. It's not going away. It's a permanent fixture in human nature. Yet its existence should not force us into a deep hole away from the world. To live a complete life, we need to unleash our true self and have trust that everything will be ok. It's a great feeling, because by trusting and being genuine, we can open ourselves up to many exciting possibilities.

That does not mean we should be naive. Regardless of the person, you should give them a basic level of trust, but simultaneously put them to the test. Do they measure up? You can relax in your true self while casually observing with your mind. It's about being alert but rested. It's about using your healthy ego to do what it was meant to; monitor what is good and what is bad for you. This monitoring should not be done with coldness, however. Dealing with narcissism is not about labelling a person and then forgetting them. It's about trying to see each new situation for what it is and then deciding if it's time to shut down or walk away. Contempt is a tool which you should only use when necessary.

Life is beautiful, and many people we come across will enrich our experience. These people in our lives could make mistakes, and they could occasionally act in hurtful (and narcissistic) ways. We all have the capacity to be cold and calculating, not just narcissists. We humans do cruel things in the name of avoiding pain and shame. But we shouldn't risk losing all that life has to offer because we shut the door too soon. We should trust, always, and we should verify. Always.

New beginnings

Just living is not enough... one must have sunshine, freedom, and a little flower.

- Hans Christian Andersen

With the seven practices, you will begin to have a stronger sense of self. You will also;

- Be able to separate yourself from your emotions, withstand them and manage them with skill
- Be able to separate other people from your emotions, and by doing so be able to shield yourself from manipulation
- Understand that each person is responsible for their own emotions
- Master your shame, allowing you to embrace your humanity and to grow as a person
- Find creative ways to express your true self
- Gain confidence and new skills
- Cultivate balanced, satisfying relationships
- Have allies to rely on when needed
- Be much more immune to subjugation and narcissism

- Explore your passion with vigour and live a life of wholeness

You'll also begin to experience peace inside, and you'll notice a space open up which didn't exist before. That space will become your fortress, not just from narcissists, but from the pressures of the world. The battle is fought around this fortress. When you stop complying with narcissists, and begin to pull away from their games by catering to your own interests, the narcissist will notice and resist this. They might react with anger and attack you with their rage. They could try one of their many tricks such as baiting or hoovering, all in the hope of gaining access to your fortress and thus resuming their manipulation. You will not allow this. This fortress will feel holy and pure, and you will feel a natural urge to protect it no matter what. Regardless what the narcissist dangles outside, no matter if they attack you with guilt or shame, despite the mind games they play; you'll want to remain in this fortress, knowing how safe and secure it feels. Ending a relationship with a narcissist, especially a destructive one, and going no contact might be necessary. This will become much easier when you have your fortress to help you weather the storm.

Coup d'état

Once you begin to slay narcissists, you may feel the need for a regime change. If so, then the next step will be to actively identify and free yourself of all narcissist regimes in your life - for good.

Even the most normal of relationships and structures can exist under the shadow of narcissism. You might need to change jobs, distance yourself from relatives, let relationships and friendships die a slow death or even wind down a business. This will happen gradually as you reinforce the seven practices.

The structures and relationships in your life will not necessarily be all bad. The questions you will need to ask yourself when considering each structure are: How oppressive is it? Do I value it? Does it allow me to be myself? Does it support my growth or does it keep me stuck in a rut? For every one of your relationships and commitments, think about who or what you are serving. Assisting your child's growth, for example, is indeed worthy, whereas serving the narcissistic needs of an aloof and uncaring boss while doing a job which you hate, is not. Sacrificing your time in order to support a narcissistic friend's hedonism might be exciting for a while, but will be nowhere near as fulfilling as sharing experiences alongside a companion as you help each other grow. You will need to establish which relationships and which structures are oppressive to your true self, and look at how you can replace them with ones that better serve you. The more you reinforce the seven practices, the louder the voice of your true self becomes. In time, it will be so loud that you will have no choice but to listen to it. Then you will act.

Out with the old, in with the new

Walking away from a narcissist regime leaves a big void. You can't underestimate the psychological effect which it will have on you. It can be both an exciting and turbulent time. Fear and uncertainty is sure to arise, but with a strong sense of self and support from your allies, it will all be manageable.

What now? you might then ask. Nobody can help you figure this out. We fight to break free from narcissism so that we finally have the right to answer that question for ourselves. The more in touch with your true self you become, the more your childhood impulses might come to life. That might be a good place to start. Some people feel a need to revisit childhood dreams and then find pragmatic ways to bring those dreams to life in adulthood. You might decide to enjoy your freedom more simply. As the floodgates open, you will know what to do.

With courage, good support and imagination, you will walk the newly open road and finally start living the life you were supposed to. When you can work creatively with what you have, the possibilities suddenly become endless. The past is done with, what comes next is completely up to you.

Revenge is a dish best not served at all

In moments of doubt and frustration, it's normal that you might want to express your anger. You may want to unleash your rage on the narcissist and give them a taste of their own medicine. On the other hand, you could decide to appeal to their humanity by telling them how they've hurt you and hope that their guilt or shame puts them in their place. You might not want to cut your losses and instead, choose to invest a bit more time trying to change the narcissist. You could give them a heartfelt speech about love, and in doing so, carry them over to the good side. You might want to save them from the horrors of their past.

Don't.

It is an enormous pill to swallow. Always remember, the narcissist doesn't play by the same rules. You can't appeal to their moral judgement. Their behaviour only changes when you start pulling away, and the minute you're back in the game, they will carry on as before. They are driven by a survival instinct, not on loving, emotional understanding. Carving out a new, independent reality gives you freedom, whereas engaging the narcissist in their games keeps you trapped in their reality.

Nothing drives a narcissist crazier than indifference. Their identity and entire sense of self are based on the reactions of others. Their energy field is invigorated with every reaction they get out of their target. Every time they pull a string and get a response, they confirm their self-declared status as overlord. Every ruse that works gives them a shot of satisfaction directly into their veins. On the other hand, having their ability to control you taken away literally feels like death for them. With each blank stare you give them, and with each firm boundary you set, you snatch their strength away from them. They will fall into an empty abyss and experience death firsthand.

Once the death of the narcissist is achieved, the focus then switches away from them and back to you and your journey. As you travel through each day, remember the law of grandiosity. Ask yourself; who am I worshiping and why? In every relationship, and in every role you play, what are you reducing yourself to? Do you allow yourself to become a sounding board? Or a servant? Do you forego what you value because you feel guilty letting others down? Do you live in an invisible prison where you feel powerless? Is that all you want from your life? Is that all you were born to be?

Your subconscious conditioning is a stubborn beast which will challenge you at every step, no doubt. You won't succeed with one blow. It takes asking these questions every single day and in every situation until the ship slowly changes direction. It takes courage and persistence. It takes the support of good people. It takes consistently remembering your true self, and doing everything in your power to stay connected to it. Through pain and joy, fear and guilt, success and failure, doubt and weakness, remember always to stick with your true self. It's the greatest ally you will ever have. Even when it doesn't come naturally, seek balance in your relationships and, instead of worshipping a false god, believe in yourself. Remember to *trust* yourself; no matter what.

After experiencing some psychological air and freedom, there might be moments when you find yourself unconsciously reverting to role playing. It might be that you were having a good day and were open enough to be unwittingly sucked back into the narcissist's ploys. You might have been feeling especially vulnerable. It happens. As always, the key is to practice a calm, relaxed vigilance, and to give yourself permission to slip up occasionally.

Most importantly, as you progress with this journey, be kind to yourself. Hold the judgements and allow your true self space to simply be. That's all it ever really wanted. Remember that you are a human being who is worthy of love and respect. You make mistakes. You have limits. You also have every right to dream big while having a responsibility to respect your fellow human. Like Superman or Superwoman, you have the potential for abundant strength. The more emotionally resilient you become, the more power you gain in your life. And just like Superman or Superwoman, you are guided by your moral compass. Superman and Superwoman know that their power and strength is a responsibility to care for others, not a license to manipulate and control. Like a tree with deep roots and fertile branches, you will be immovable while still offering your fruit to those who seek mutual love. That is the path to strong living. That is the art of killing a narcissist.

Resources

Healing The Shame That Binds You - John Bradshaw
https://www.amazon.com/Healing-Shame-Binds-Recovery-Classics/dp/0757303234

Rubber Shoes In Hell - An honest, raw blog by a survivor of parental narcissism
http://www.rubbershoesinhell.com/category/narcissism/

Voicelessness - Essays on narcissism by Richard Grossman
http://www.voicelessness.com/essay.html

Conversational Narcissism - A fascinating article on talking with narcissists
http://www.artofmanliness.com/2011/05/01/the-art-of-conversation-how-to-avoid-conversational-narcissism/

An informative article on the importance of limbic resonance
http://attachmentdisorderhealing.com/therapy-love/

Narcissists who cry - Playing the victim

http://psychcentral.com/blog/archives/2010/03/29/
narcissists-who-cry-the-other-side-of-the-ego/

**Shut up and be patient - A crude, slightly forceful
yet fantastic read. Very useful when you feel like
you're stuck and change is not happening.
(Warning: Explicit)**
http://markmanson.net/be-patient

**Odd friendships - An article on becoming aware of
unhelpful friendship dynamics**
http://waitbutwhy.com/2014/12/10-types-odd-friendships-
youre-probably-part.html

**The continuum of self - A fascinating companion to
the shame/grandiosity continuum**
http://humanmagnetsyndrome.com/blog/
2016/08/27/3345/

In-depth resources on narcissism by Sam Vaknin
http://samvak.tripod.com/

Toxic venting - When to stop listening
http://www.huffingtonpost.com/judith-acosta/toxic-
venting_b_822505.html

Made in the USA
San Bernardino, CA
18 July 2018